C000157148

Isaac Watts

Isaac Watts

Holiness and Happiness

The Piety of Isaac Watts

introduced and edited by
W. Britt Stokes

Reformation Heritage Books
Grand Rapids, Michigan

Holiness and Happiness
© 2022 by W. Britt Stokes

All rights reserved. No part of this book may be used or reproduced in any manner whatsoever without written permission except in the case of brief quotations embodied in critical articles and reviews. Direct your requests to the publisher at the following addresses:

Reformation Heritage Books
3070 29th St. SE
Grand Rapids, MI 49512
616–977–0889
orders@heritagebooks.org
www.heritagebooks.org

Scripture taken from the King James Version. In the public domain.

Printed in the United States of America
22 23 24 25 26 27/10 9 8 7 6 5 4 3 2 1

Library of Congress Cataloging-in-Publication Data

Names: Stokes, W. Britt, author.
Title: Holiness and happiness : the piety of Isaac Watts / introduced and edited by W. Britt Stokes.
Description: Grand Rapids, Michigan : Reformation Heritage Books, [2022] | Includes bibliographical references.
Identifiers: LCCN 2022024259 (print) | LCCN 2022024260 (ebook) | ISBN 9781601789617 (paperback) | ISBN 9781601789624 (epub)
Subjects: LCSH: Watts, Isaac, 1674-1748. | Piety. | Holiness—Christianity. | Theology, Doctrinal—England—17th century—History. | Church of England—Doctrines. | BISAC: RELIGION / Christian Living / Spiritual Growth | RELIGION / Christian Living / General
Classification: LCC BX5207.W3 S76 2022 (print) | LCC BX5207.W3 (ebook) | DDC 202/.2—dc23/eng/20220718
LC record available at https://lccn.loc.gov/2022024259
LC ebook record available at https://lccn.loc.gov/2022024260

For additional Reformed literature, request a free book list from Reformation Heritage Books at the above regular or e-mail address.

PROFILES IN REFORMED SPIRITUALITY

series editors—Joel R. Beeke and Michael A. G. Haykin

Dustin W. Benge, *"Sweetly Set on God": The Piety of David Brainerd*

Andrew S. Ballitch and J. Stephen Yuille, *"The Wholesome Doctrine of the Gospel": Faith and Love in the Writings of William Perkins*

Nathan A. Finn and Aaron Lumpkin, *"The Sum and Substance of the Gospel": The Christ-Centered Piety of Charles Haddon Spurgeon*

Table of Contents

Section Three
The Cultivation of Piety

Profiles in Reformed Spirituality

Charles Dickens's famous line in *A Tale of Two Cities*—
"It was the best of times, it was the worst of times"
—seems well suited to Western evangelicalism since
the 1960s. On the one hand, these decades have seen
much for which to praise God and to rejoice. In His
goodness and grace, for instance, Reformed truth is
no longer a house under siege. Growing numbers
identify themselves theologically with what we hold
to be biblical truth, namely, Reformed theology and
piety. And yet, as an increasing number of Reformed
authors have noted, there are many sectors of the
surrounding Western evangelicalism that are charac-
terized by great shallowness and a trivialization of the
weighty things of God. So much of evangelical worship seems barren. And when it comes to spirituality,
there is little evidence of the riches of our heritage as
Reformed evangelicals.

As it was at the time of the Reformation, when the
watchword was *ad fontes*—"back to the sources"—so
it is now: The way forward is backward. We need to
go back to the spiritual heritage of Reformed evangelicalism to find the pathway forward. We cannot live
in the past; to attempt to do so would be antiquarian-
ism. But our Reformed forebearers in the faith can
teach us much about Christianity, its doctrines, its
passions, and its fruit.

And they can serve as our role models. As R. C. Sproul has noted of such giants as Augustine, Martin Luther, John Calvin, and Jonathan Edwards: "These men all were conquered, overwhelmed, and spiritually intoxicated by their vision of the holiness of God. Their minds and imaginations were captured by the majesty of God the Father. Each of them possessed a profound affection for the sweetness and excellence of Christ. There was in each of them a singular and unswerving loyalty to Christ that spoke of a citizenship in heaven that was always more precious to them than the applause of men."[1]

To be sure, we would not dream of placing these men and their writings alongside the Word of God. John Jewel (1522–1571), the Anglican apologist, once stated: "What say we of the fathers, Augustine, Ambrose, Jerome, Cyprian?... They were learned men, and learned fathers; the instruments of the mercy of God, and vessels full of grace. We despise them not, we read them, we reverence them, and give thanks unto God for them. Yet...we may not make them the foundation and warrant of our conscience: we may not put our trust in them. Our trust is in the name of the Lord."[2]

Seeking, then, both to honor the past and yet not idolize it, we are issuing these books in the series Profiles in Reformed Spirituality. The design is to introduce the spirituality and piety of the Reformed

---

1. R. C. Sproul, "An Invaluable Heritage," *Tabletalk* 23, no. 10 (October 1999): 5–6.

2. Cited in Barrington R. White, "Why Bother with History?," *Baptist History and Heritage* 4, no. 2 (July 1969): 85.

tradition by presenting descriptions of the lives of notable Christians with select passages from their works. This combination of biographical sketches and collected portions from primary sources gives a taste of the subjects' contributions to our spiritual heritage and some direction as to how the reader can find further edification through their works. It is the hope of the publisher that this series will provide riches for those areas where we are poor and light of day where we are stumbling in the deepening twilight.

—Joel R. Beeke
Michael A. G. Haykin

The Life and Piety of Isaac Watts
(1674–1748)

Isaac Watts was born in Southampton, England, on July 17, 1674, the oldest of eight siblings. At the time of Watts's birth and during his younger years, deep ecclesiological tensions existed within the Church of England. In 1662 Parliament passed the Act of Uniformity, which, among other things, formally enforced conformity to the Church of England and its liturgy.[1] As a result, some two thousand ministers left the Church of England and became what is known as nonconformists or dissenters.

Watts's immediate relatives, particularly his father, Isaac Watts Sr., were deeply committed to the nonconformist cause. His family belonged to an Independent congregation that was pastored by the

---

1. For more on the Act of Uniformity, see N. H. Keeble, *"Settling the Peace of the Church": 1662 Revisited* (New York: Oxford University Press, 2014); Michael Watts, *The Dissenters* (Oxford: Clarendon Press, 1978); George Gould, ed., *Documents Relating to the Settlement of the Church of England by the Act of Uniformity of 1662* (London: W. Kent, 1862); Peter Bayne, "English Puritanism: Its Character and History," in *Documents Relating to the Settlement of the Church of England by the Act of Uniformity of 1662*, ed. George Gould (London: W. Kent, 1862), 1–142; and Edmund Calamy, *An Account of the Ministers, Lecturers, Masters and Fellows of Colleges and Schoolmasters, Who were Ejected or Silenced after the Restoration in 1660…*(London: J. Lawrence, J. Nicholson, and J. Sprint, 1713).

ejected rector Nathaniel Robinson.[2] Watts's father
was a deacon and trustee, as well as the leaseholder
to the property.[3] He was known as "a man of strong
convictions…[who] was willing to suffer for the
sake of his conscience."[4] The senior Watts was frequently persecuted and even imprisoned because of
his nonconformity. In a document entitled "Memo-
rable Affair in My Life," the younger Watts (at nine
years of age) noted his father's 1683 imprisonment
for nonconformity.[5] Two years later, while fleeing
Southampton to evade persecution, Watts Sr. penned
a letter to his children that gives an indication of his
fatherly piety. He wrote,

> Though it hath pleased the only wise God to
> suffer the malice of ungodly men, the enemies
> of Jesus Christ (and my enemies for his sake),
> to break out so far against me, as to remove me
> from you in my personal habitation, thereby
> at once bereaving me of that comfort, which I
> might have hoped for in the enjoyment of my
> family in peace, and you of that education,
> which my love as a father and duty as a parent
> required me to give; yet such are the longings of
> my soul for your good and prosperity, especially
> in spiritual concernments, that I remember

---

2. Watts's oldest brother, Richard (1676–1750), was a prosperous
London physician. A second brother, Enoch (b. 1680), was involved
with the first biography of Watts by Gibbons. For very brief details on
the other siblings, see Arthur P. Davis, *Isaac Watts: His Life and Works*
(London: Independent Press, 1943), 6–7.

3. Davis, *Isaac Watts*, 4.

4. Davis, *Isaac Watts*, 4.

5. Davis, *Isaac Watts*, 5.

you always with myself in my daily prayers addressed to the throne of grace.[6]

As the master of a local boarding school in Southampton, the elder Watts was keenly attuned to the spiritual and educational growth of his children. In a letter in 1685, the elder Watts provided six "lines of counsel" for his children related to the Christian faith. They included the following: (1) frequent reading of the Holy Scriptures; (2) serious consideration for their "sinful and miserable estate...by nature"; (3) pursuing knowledge of God by His "glorious attributes and infinite perfections," especially by way of the Lord Jesus Christ; (4) remembering God as their Creator; (5) worshiping God "according to the rules of the gospel"; and (6) being "dutiful and obedient to all your superiors."[7] The strong religious influence of his family is seen in an acrostic Watts wrote at age seven:

> I am a vile polluted lump of earth,
> So I've continued ever since my birth,
> Although Jehovah grace does daily give me,
> As sure this monster Satan will deceive me,
> Come therefore, Lord, from Satan's claws
>   relieve me.
>
> Wash me in Thy blood, O Christ,
> And grace divine impart,
> Then search and try the corners of my heart,

6. David G. Fountain, *Isaac Watts Remembered*, 2nd ed. (Harpenden, England: Gospel Standard Trust, 1978), 17.

7. Fountain, *Isaac Watts Remembered*, 17–19.

That I in all things may be fit to do
Service to thee, and sing thy praises too.[8]

As a result of the faithful witness of his family, Watts realized the rich contents of the gospel message at a young age. These early theological moorings would remain throughout the balance of his faithful life and ministry. While Watts Sr. was a strong spiritual influence, the father's artistic and poetic bent also shaped his son.[9] Two stanzas of his poem "The Soul's Desire of Remove," written when he was eighty-five, demonstrate his abilities:

Worn with the tils of fourscore years and five,
A weary pilgrim, Lord, to thee I come;
To beg supporting grace, till I arrive
At heaven, thy promis'd rest, my wish'd-for
     home.

Here's nothing to invite my longer stay,
Among the darksome melancholy cells;

---

8. Thomas Gibbons, *Memoirs of Isaac Watts* (London: James Buckland and Thomas Gibbons, 1780), 5.

9. The earliest record of Watts's family is regarding his grandfather Thomas Watts. Thomas was a gifted man, and, like Isaac, his interest and abilities spanned all sorts of disciplines. In a lyrical poem written in 1693 on the death of "Mrs. M. W.," who was an "honored relative" of Watts, he included a footnote to one of the stanzas about his grandfather. Watts notes, "My grandfather Mr. Thomas Watts had such acquaintance with the mathematics, painting, music and poesy, &c. as gave him considerable esteem among his contemporaries. He was commander of a ship of war 1656, and by blowing up the ship in the Dutch war he was drowned in his youth." See Isaac Watts, *The Works of the Late Reverend and Learned Isaac Watts...*(London: J. Barfield, 1810), 4:494.

When shall I leave this tenement of clay?
Fain would I be where my Redeemer dwells.

This poem clearly shows the lineage of a talent for poetry writing that would pass to the younger Watts.

The lasting godly influence of Watts's family played a critical role in his life and was influential in his conversion. Accordingly, he struggled with "considerable convictions of sin" before coming to a saving knowledge of Christ in 1688 at the age of fourteen.[10]

School Years

Watts's educational bent was apparent at a very young age. He was described as "the little Puritan [who] was the most diligent and advanced scholar, the beloved of his master."[11] At age four, Watts had begun to learn Latin from his father. At age seven, he began to learn Greek. By the time he reached thirteen, he had learned Hebrew and French.[12] A "pale child," there was "certainly nothing robust about him, but [he had] all the indications of the future scholar."[13] His formal education began in 1680, at age six, when he was sent to grammar school at the Free-School at Southampton. It was there he received an excellent education by studying under the direction

---

10. Davis, *Isaac Watts*, 8.

11. Edwin Paxton Hood, *Isaac Watts: His Life and Writings, His Homes and Friends* (London: Religious Tract Society, 1875), 8.

12. Davis, *Isaac Watts*, 8.

13. Hood, *Isaac Watts: His Life and Writings*, 8.

of John Pinhorne (1652–1714).[14] Pinhorne had a deep
influence on Watts, and they shared a close bond, for
which Watts's loyalty and thankfulness was lasting.[15]

At sixteen, it was time for Watts to depart
the tutelage of Pinhorne for higher education, yet
challenges existed. One biographer notes how the
"persecutions to which the Nonconformist through
this period were exposed of course affected society
in Southampton; the avenues of prosperity and peace
seemed to lie only in conformity to the Church of
England."[16] As such, a Southampton town physician, John Speed, offered to send Watts to one of
the English universities and subsidize the expenses.
Ultimately, Watts would decline the offer and "take
up his lot amongst the Dissenters."[17] In 1690 Watts
enrolled at an institution for learning associated with
the dissenters of the age, Thomas Rowe's Academy
in London. His esteem and affection for Rowe were
much the same as he had had for his earlier teacher,
Pinhorne. Watts wrote a lyrical poem to Rowe,
which in part reads,

I love thy gentle influence, Rowe,
Thy gentle influence like the sun,

---

14. Davis, *Isaac Watts*, 8. Pinhorne was the master of the Free-
School at Southampton, rector of All-Saints in Southampton, and
vicar of the parish Eling in Hampshire, England.

15. Watts's affection for Pinhorne was so strong that he wrote a
lyrical poem in Latin as an ode to him. For the Latin and English
translation of the lyrical poem, see Gibbons, *Memoirs of Isaac Watts*,
7–19.

16. Hood, *Isaac Watts: His Life and Writings*, 13.

17. Hood, *Isaac Watts: His Life and Writings*, 14.

Only dissolves the frozen snow,
Then bids our thoughts like rivers flow.[18]

Even in these formative years at Rowe's Academy, the young Watts produced works pertaining to theology, metaphysics, and ethics.[19] Furthermore, his gift for writing poetry continued to emerge during his studies there.[20] In 1694, at the age of twenty, Watts formally ended his academic career and returned to his father's house in Southampton.[21] For a two-year period, Watts spent time in "reading, meditation, and prayer" in order to prepare "for that work [the ministry] to which he was determined to devote his life."[22]

Ministry Years

At the end of his years of preparation, Watts accepted a position as tutor in the home of Sir John Hartopp in Stoke Newington. After five years of tutoring, he formally entered the ministry, accepting the position

---

18. Gibbons, *Memoirs of Isaac Watts*, 20.

19. Watts's brother Enoch left two volumes of manuscripts to the biographer Thomas Gibbons. The two volumes contained twenty-two Latin dissertations penned by Watts during his academic career at Rowe's Academy. For the transcript of two of Watts's Latin theses, see Gibbons, *Memoirs of Isaac Watts*, 21–37.

20. Some of Watts's poetry from this period is in letters to his family. For a specific sample of the poetry Watts wrote during his time at the Academy, see the letter to his brother Richard, dated 1692, in Gibbons, *Memoirs of Isaac Watts*, 69–71.

21. In 1728 the University of Edinburgh and the University of Aberdeen conferred on Watts honorary doctorate degrees. See David Jennings, *A Sermon Occasioned by the Death of the Late Reverend Isaac Watts D.D…December 11, 1748* (London: J. Oswald and W. Dilly, 1749), 26–27.

22. See Gibbons, *Memoirs of Isaac Watts*, 92.

of associate pastor at Mark Lane Congregational
Chapel in London.[23] On March 18, 1702, Watts
succeeded Isaac Chauncy (1632–1712) as pastor. He
accepted this call immediately following Chauncy's
resignation in January 1702. Thomas Rowe's church
provided a letter of recommendation for Watts:

> For as much as our dear brother Mr. Isaac
> Watts who was with great satisfaction admit-
> ted a member amongst us, and hath since
> walked as becomes the gospel to the glory of
> God and to the honour of his holy profession,
> doth now desire his dismission from us, we do
> in compliance therewith discharge him from
> his membership among us in order to his being
> received by you, praying that his ministerial
> labours, and those gifts and graces wherewith
> the Lord Jesus Christ, the great head of the
> church, hath been pleased so richly to furnish
> him may be abundantly blessed to the conver-
> sion of souls, and your edification, to whose
> grace and blessing we do from our hearts com-
> mend both him and you.[24]

Because of recurring illness, Watts was absent
from the pulpit for prolonged periods. His health
became such an issue that the church eventually hired
Samuel Price to serve as an assistant. In September
1712, Watts suffered from a particularly difficult
illness. He was "seized with a violent fever which

---

23. Watts preached his first sermon on July 17, 1698, on his
twenty-fourth birthday.
24. Watts, *Works*, 1:xiv; and Gibbons, *Memoirs of Isaac Watts*,
97–98.

shook his constitution and left such wakens upon his nerves as continued with him in some degree to his dying day."[25] This illness kept Watts from engaging in public ministry until 1716. As such, in 1713, Price was formally ordained as the copastor of Mark Lane for the rest of the time of Watts's extended illness. Eventually Watts took residence in the home of Thomas Abney and lived there for thirty-six years. During this period Watts continued to pastor, teach, and write. Also, he remained unmarried. The move to the Abney residence was always understood as deeply providential by Watts in light of his illnesses. The impact of the Abneys' kindness toward Watts was tremendous. One early biographer captures the nature and importance of the Abney family to Watts:

> Here he enjoyed the uninterrupted demonstrations of the truest friendship. Here, without any care of his own, he had everything which could contribute to the enjoyment of life, and favour the unwearied pursuit of his studies. Here he dwelt in a family which for piety, order, harmony, and every virtue was a house of God. Here he had the privilege of a country recess, the pure air, the retired grove, the fragrant bower, the spreading lawn, the flowery garden, and other advantages to sooth his mind, an aid to his restoration to health, to yield him whenever he chose them most grateful intervals from his laborious studies, and enable him to return to them with doubled vigour and delight.[26]

---

25. Gibbons, *Memoirs of Isaac Watts*, 100.
26. Gibbons, *Memoirs of Isaac Watts*, 113.

Watts's writing is often believed to be the most defining part of his life as he was "obligated…to pass the most of his time in retirement from the world" because of his bouts of illness.[27] Watts's friends Philip Doddridge and David Jennings, who would compile and publish the first edition of his works after his death, recognized this. In the preface to the first volume of these works, they note that "the Doctor's feeble state of health, through the greater part of his life…[caused] not so many incidents and changes…as generally furnished out a good part of such histories."[28]

Watts longed for his character to be understood in light of the works he produced and published. He demonstrated this in his desire not to have his personal letters published after his death. When others asked that he "leave some memoirs that might furnish out such a history [of his life], he absolutely declined it; and desired that his character might stand in the world merely as it would appear in his works."[29] This disposition gave way to Watts's devotion to writing. He published numerous poems and hymns: *Horae Lyricae* (1706) and *Hymns and Spiritual Songs* (1707).[30] Some of his most influential works

---

27. Philip Doddridge and David Jennings, preface to *The Works of the Late Reverend and Learned Isaac Watts, D.D…*(London: T. and T. Longman, and J. Buckland; J. Oswald; J. Waugh; and J. Ward, 1753), 1:iii.

28. Doddridge and Jennings, preface, 1:iii.

29. See Doddridge and Jennings, preface, 1:iii.

30. For more on Watts's poetry, psalms, and hymns, see Harry Escott, *Isaac Watts, Hymnographer: A Study of the Beginnings, Development and Philosophy of the English Hymn* (London: Independent Press,

were related to education: *Logic* (1724) and *Improvement of the Mind* (1741). He also wrote on a vast array of subjects such as civics, metaphysics, and astronomy,[31] and he penned several practical works for the common Christian: among them, *A Guide to Prayer* (1715) and *An Humble Attempt towards the Revival of Practical Religion* (1731).

The popularity of Watts's works extended well beyond England. Cotton Mather is credited with first introducing Watts's hymns to New England as appendices to both printed sermons and written guides to prayer.[32] According to historical data from an eighteenth-century society that distributed printed material to the poor, Watts's *Hymns and Spiritual Songs* (1707), *Divine Songs for Children* (1715), *Psalms of David* (1719), *Prayers for the Use of Children* (1728), *Short View of the Whole Scripture History* (1732), and *First and Second Set of Catechisms* (1730) "reached a larger audience than all other books including the Bible."[33]

1962); Donald Davie, *The Eighteenth-Century Hymn in England* (New York: Cambridge University Press, 1993); and J. R. Watson, *The English Hymn: A Critical and Historical Study* (New York: Oxford University Press, 1999).

31. For a detailed discussion of each publication, see Watts, *Works*, 1:xix–xxxvii. For a chronological list of Watts's works, see Thomas Milner, *The Life, Times and Correspondence of the Rev. Isaac Watts, D.D.* (London: Simpkin and Marshall, 1834), xvii–xxi.

32. Christopher N. Phillips, "Cotton Mather Brings Isaac Watts's Hymns to America; or, How to Perform a Hymn without Singing It," *The New England Quarterly* 85, no. 2 (June 2012): 205–10.

33. Isabel Rivers, "The First Evangelical Tract Society," *Historical Journal* 50, no.1 (March 2007): 8–9.

Approach to the Spiritual Life

Another important part of Watts's legacy is his approach to the spiritual life. Watts was deeply concerned about piety, and his approach to the spiritual life has impacted scores of Christians on both sides of the Atlantic for many decades. Though his hymns are ordinarily considered the center of his true genius

A statue of Watts currently located in Watts Park (West), Southampton, Hampshire, England

and piety, Watts was also a pastor, philosopher, and theologian. His entire corpus of writing is richly spiritual and deeply committed to practical Christian piety. Esther Edwards Burr, the daughter of Jonathan and Sarah Edwards, helps capture the uniquely pious nature of Watts's writings in her journal: "Since Mr. Burr [her husband] left me I have been reading Dr. Watts's Miscellaneous thoughts, which I have never read before. I think them like the rest of that valuable gentleman's works. There is something in the good Doctor's writings different from everybody else—more engaging."[34]

The main feature of Watts's approach to the spiritual life is his emphasis on holiness and happiness. He believed holiness and happiness are "eternal life begun" for the Christian. In other words, Watts argues that the life of piety is devoted to the pursuit of holiness and happiness, which begins in part on earth and is fulfilled in heaven. Holiness and happiness are principally spiritual matters, grounded in the soul and built on Christian doctrine. Three key doctrines provide clarity on how Watts arrives at holiness and happiness as the basis for his piety.

The first doctrine is the depravity of man. Original sin pervades humanity. Watts writes, "What tongue can express, or what heart can conceive, the immense load; and everlasting train of mischiefs and miseries, that lie heavy on poor mankind...for almost six thousand years? All these were introduced

---

34. Esther Edwards Burr, *The Journal of Esther Edwards Burr 1754–1757*, ed. Carol F. Karlsen and Laurie Crumpacker (New Haven, Conn.: Yale University Press, 1984), 45.

by man's first disobedience."[35] Watts believes there
are two types of people on earth: the natural man
and the spiritual man. The natural man rejects the
"two chief spirits...God and his own soul" while
taking "pains to gratify [his] senses, and indulge
every fleshly appetite."[36] Conversely, the spiritual
man is one who pursues holiness and attempts to
"mortify [his] sinful passions and set [his] affection
on things above."[37]

The second doctrine is the work of Christ. Given
humanity's predicament, Christ alone is the way to
happiness and holiness. Christ secures both by means
of His mediatorial work. This is on full display in
Watts's writings as he continually points us to the
Christocentric nature of true Christian piety.

The third doctrine is the excellency of heaven.
Watts viewed death as the doorway to the ultimate
experience of holiness and happiness—eternal life.
Without this hope, there is no holiness or happiness
in the present. He goes as far as to suggest that the
pursuit of holiness and happiness is the means by
which the Christian prepares for eternity. It is the
"noblest honour" and the "sweetest consolation" of
every Christian to "get as near [God] as earth and
grace will admit" because "[holiness and happiness

---

35. Watts, *Works*, 1:125; Isaac Watts, *Sermons on Various Subjects*
(London: Printed for John Clark, E. M. Matthews, and Richard Ford,
1721), 1:358.

36. Watts, *Works*, 1:39; and Watts, *Sermons on Various Subjects*,
1:107.

37. Watts, *Works*, 1:39; and Watts, *Sermons on Various Subjects*,
1:107–8.

are] the best preparative for heaven and the state of glory."[38]

Watts exhorts the believer to deepen holiness and happiness through love for and knowledge of God. First, he maintains that knowledge of God is foundational because in order to experience God, the mind must know Him. He explains, "It is impossible that we should love anything that we know not: and it is not to be expected that we should love God supremely or with all our heart, if we have not known him to be more excellent, and more desirable than all other things we are acquainted with."[39] The mind, therefore, is critical to the pursuit of holiness and happiness. Second, the Christian cultivates holiness and happiness through love for God. As Christians grow in the knowledge of God, they also grow in their appreciation of God's love.[40] This, in turn, compels them to love God. Watts asserts that God is the "first cause" of love and "must be the last end of all, and no creatures, as divided from him, can make us either holy or happy."[41] According to Watts, love and knowledge are then practically cultivated through meditation, prayer, worship, the Lord's Supper, friendship, and Christian virtue.

---

38. Watts, *Works*, 1:130; and Watts, *Sermons on Various Subjects*, 1:372.

39. Watts, *Works*, 2:637; and Isaac Watts, *Discourses of the Love of God and the Use and Abuse of the Passion in Religion, with a Devout Meditation Suited to Each Discourse*…(London: J. Clark, R. Hett, E. Matthews, and R. Ford, 1729), 110.

40. Watts, *Works*, 2:638; and Watts, *Discourses of the Love of God*, 110–11.

41. Watts, *Works*, 1:124; and Watts, *Sermons on Various Subjects*, 1:357.

Isaac Watts's grave site at
Bunhill Fields Burial Grounds in London

Conclusion

Watts's concern for godliness was ever present throughout his entire life. A firsthand account of his final days notes that he had "the least shadow of a doubt as to his future everlasting happiness."[42] He passed into eternal glory on November 25, 1748. In the sermon for Watts's funeral, David Jennings spoke of his piety, remarking, "The active and sprightly powers of his nature failed him...yet his trust in God, through Jesus the Mediator, remained unshaken to the last."[43]

---

42. Gibbons, *Memoirs of Isaac Watts*, 314.

43. David Jennings, *A Sermon Occasioned by the Death of the Late Reverend Isaac Watts D.D.* (London: J. Oswald and W. Dilly, 1749), 33.

SECTION ONE

The Nature of Piety

1

Aversion to Sin

Holiness consists in an aversion to and hatred of all sin. This is complete in heaven, and without this, heaven cannot be complete. Into heaven there enters nothing "that defileth" (Rev. 21:27). Every inhabitant there is completely averse to all iniquity and hates everything that displeases God. For nothing but perfect obedience is found there; the spirits of the just are there made perfect (Heb. 7:23). Now this in a measure and degree is found in believers here, for he who abides in Christ "sinneth not" (1 John 3:6). He cannot sin with a full purpose of heart. He who is born of God cannot sin with constancy and greediness, as others do who are only born of flesh and blood. He cannot sin without an inward sincere reluctance, without the combat of the spirit against the flesh. He does not make a trade of sin; sinning is not his business, his delight, and pleasure. This is a blessed testimony of the truth of the gospel, that faith in the Son of God purifies the heart (Acts 15:9).

Every Christian has an aversion to all sin. If he chooses some sins to continue in and hates other iniquities, he can never be said to be a true believer in Christ and to have the work of faith in sincerity wrought in his heart.

Other religions have professed an aversion to some sins but indulged others. Some make cruelty a part of their duty and require the sacrificing of mankind to appease the anger of their gods—a bloody and impious practice, as well as a vain and fruitless one! Some forbid murder but allow and encourage a variety of uncleanness and make that a part of their worship. Other professions have forbid wanton practices and commended chastity, but they indulge resentment and revenge as a necessary part of the character of a warrior or a great man. Carnal and sensual lusts have been opposed and hated by some of the old philosophers, but spiritual iniquities have hereby been promoted. Pride has hereby been wonderfully increased, and none of them can excuse themselves from those sins that make men very like Satan, although they are freed from the brutality of sensual lusts. But the business of the gospel of Christ is to keep men from committing any kind of sins whatsoever.*

---

* Watts, *Works*, 1:12.

John Flavel (ca. 1627–1691)

English Puritan pastor-theologian whom Watts held in high regard. Watts used Flavel's thought and writings in many of his own works.

2

Above This World

If we look upward to heaven, we will behold there all the inhabitants looking down with a sacred contempt on the trifles, amusements, businesses, and cares of this present life that engross our affections, awaken our desires, and fill our hearts with pleasure or pain and our flesh with constant labor. With what holy scorn do you think those souls, who are dismissed from flesh, look down on the hurries and bustles of this present state in which we are engaged? They dwell in the full sight of those glories that they hoped for here on earth, and their intimate acquaintance with the pleasures of that upper world and the divine sensations that are raised in them there make them condemn all the pleasures of this state and everything below heaven. This is a part of eternal life.

This belongs in some degree to every believer, for he is not a believer who is not got above this world in a good measure. He is not a Christian who is not weaned in some degree from this world, for this is our victory whereby we overcome the world, even our faith. He who is born of God overcomes the world; he who believes in Jesus is born of God (1 John 5:1–4). From this the argument is plain: the one who believes in Jesus, the Son of God, overcomes this present world.

And where Christianity is raised to a good degree of life and power in the soul, there we see the Christian got near to heaven. He is, as it were, a fellow for angels, a fit companion for the spirits of the just made perfect. The affairs of this life are beneath his best desires and his hopes. He engages his hand in them as far as God his Father appoints his duty, but he longs for the upper world, where his hopes are gone before: "When will I be entirely dismissed from this labor and toil? The gaudy pleasures this world entertains me with are no entertainments to me. I am weaned from them; I am born from above." This is the language of the faith that overcomes the world. And faith, where it is wrought in truth in the soul, has, in some measure, this effect. And where it shines in its brightness, it has, in a great degree, this sublime grace accompanying it—or rather (shall I say?) this piece of heavenly glory.

Pain and sickness, poverty and reproach, sorrow and death itself have been condemned by those who have believed in Christ Jesus with much more honor to Christianity than ever was brought to other religions by the same profession and the same practice.[*]

---

[*] Watts, *Works*, 1:13–14.

3

Enjoyment of God

Another part of the holiness of eternal life consists in a delight in the worship and enjoyment of God. This is perfect in heaven; this is eternal life. They are before the throne of God night and day—that is, perpetually—and serve Him there in His temple (Rev. 7:15). Now the Christian religion attains this end in a good measure; it brings the soul to delight in divine worship and converse with God, which no mere human religion could ever do. For since no human religion could ever teach an awakened sinner how he might appear in the presence of a holy God with assurance and comfort, no other religion could make a soul delight in the worship of God.

We can never delight in drawing near to God, who has infinite vengeance in Him, while we don't know if He will pour out that vengeance on us. We fly far from Him unless we have some good ground of hope that He will forgive us our iniquities and receive us into His favor. Now since there is no other doctrine that shows us how our sins may be forgiven or how the favor of God may be attained, there is no other religion that can allure or draw us into the presence of God with pleasure. Let us draw near and worship the Father in full assurance and confidence that He will accept our persons and our worship since we have such a High Priest to introduce us with acceptance. Since by His flesh and incarnation He has made a way for us to come into the presence of God with satisfaction and pleasure, therefore let us draw near and worship Him (Heb. 10:19–20).

The influence of this argument has been found by Christians—by every Christian—for there is not one who has believed in Christ but has had this witness in himself. There is a sweet serenity and calmness of spirit that belong to the souls of those in whom faith is lively and strong, even when they stand before God, though He is a God of terror and vengeance to sinners. For they know Jesus is their atonement, their introducer, their peace, and therefore they love to draw near to Him as a God reconciled; they rejoice in Him as their highest happiness.

Other professions of men, when they abandoned sensual pleasures and the vanities of this world, yet taught them that their happiness must flow from themselves and made their own virtues their heaven, without any regard to God. These philosophers were self-sufficient, full of themselves, and they were so far from making their rivers of pleasure to flow from the right hand of God that they even denied their dependence on Him in this respect. And they supposed their wise men to be equal with God, deriving all their blessedness from within themselves. But Christianity leads the soul out of itself to God, as it gives a clearer and larger knowledge of God Himself, in His felicitating perfections, than the heathens could ever attain. It assures us that being near to God is our heaven, and the sight of Him is our happiness, as well as provides a new and living way of access to Him through the death and resurrection of Jesus Christ. Therefore the believer rejoices in all opportunities of drawing near to God, for it is the beginning of his heaven, and his delight in it is an inward and powerful witness to the truth of his religion.[*]

---

[*] Watts, *Works*, 1:16.

4

Zeal for God

Zeal and activity for the service of God are another part of heaven, another part of eternal life and the holiness of it. We have abundant reason to believe that heaven is not a state of mere enjoyment, inactive and idle, but a state of service and activity for that God whose we are and from whom we have received infinite favors. The angels in heaven are swift messengers to perform the will of their God (Ps. 103:20–21). The spirits of just men made perfect are like angels. They do the will of God as a pattern for us on earth, for we are taught to pray that His will may be done on earth as it is in heaven. What particular services they are employed in of God we know not, but that they are forever zealous in those services which God employs them in we doubt not, we cannot disbelieve. And this active zeal in the service of God and pursuit of His glory is the very temper and practice of the true Christian, and that not only in some more important enterprises but in the common actions of life. Whether he eat or drink or whatsoever he does, he makes it his rule of life to do all to the glory of God (1 Cor. 10:31).

Now this sublime zeal, this noble activity for the service of God and His glory, was not found among the professors of other religions. To glorify God was not their aim and end; those who rose highest among the old philosophers had not set their aim and end right. Those who knew God glorified Him not as God (Rom. 1:21). They did not make the glory of God the great design of their actions. It was not zeal for God that animated them to pursue virtue but merely their own ends, their own satisfaction or ease, the vanity of their own minds, pride and attempt of superiority above other men, or, at best, their motives of action were the reasonableness of virtue and the benefit of it to themselves and their fellow citizens. But the glory of God is the aim of Christians and the end of every true believer. He has some degree of zeal for the honor of God and therefore is active in those duties that God proposes to him.

When we see a person, regardless of all his self-interests in the world and at the same time pursuing the honor of an invisible God, following hard after the glory of that God whom his fleshly eyes have not seen, we may say he has something above what mere corrupt nature leads him to or impresses on him. The believer has this witness in himself, zeal and activity for the glory of God in the world.[*]

---

[*] Watts, *Works*, 1:16–17.

5

Love for the Saints

The last thing that goes to make up holiness is a hearty love to all men, and especially to the saints. This is a noble ingredient of eternal life. This is a divine and heavenly temper. This is a beautiful part of the image of God communicated to the soul of man. That God who is the original and foundation of eternal life is a glorious pattern of this love. He makes His sun to rise and His rain to fall on the just and on the unjust and leaves not Himself without witness of His divinity by filling the hearts of men with food and gladness (see Matt. 5:45; Acts 14:17). He shows His love to enemies and rebels in forgiving millions of offenses and pardoning crimes of the largest size and deepest aggravations, and He loves His saints with peculiar tenderness. Our Lord Jesus Christ, who also is the true God and eternal life, came down from heaven to exemplify His divine love. It was His love to mankind that persuaded Him to put on flesh and blood and prevailed with Him to suffer pains, agonies, and death, that His enemies might obtain salvation and life. O glorious example of love!

Now this is in some measure wrought into the make of every true Christian and imitated in the practice of every true believer. He is obliged by one of the chief rules of his religion to love his neighbor as himself—that is, to do to others what he thinks just and reasonable that they should do to him (Matt. 22:39; Luke 6:31). He is bound to forgive freely those who offend him, as he hopes for forgiveness of his offenses against God (Matt. 6:14–15). He rejoices in the welfare of his fellow creatures without repining. He loves his enemies, does good to those who hate him, blesses those who curse him, and prays for his persecutors and spiteful foes (Luke 6:27). He pities all who are miserable but takes a peculiar delight in his fellow Christians (the Christians must be known by this, that they love one another). He does good to all, but especially to the household of faith (Gal. 6:10).*

---

* Watts, *Works*, 1:17–18.

George Whitefield (1714–1770)

The eighteenth-century revivalist was an acquaintance of Watts, and they often communicated in person and through letters.

6

Happiness Is
Nearness to God

Is nearness to God the foundation of the creature's felicity? Then how vain are all pretenses to happiness while man is a stranger to God! Let him be surrounded with all imaginable delights of sense, or let him be furnished with all advantages of reason or natural knowledge to entertain the mind, yet if he is far off from God, he must be far off from blessedness. Without God and without hope is the character of the sinful world. Do the profane and sensual wretches boast of their pleasures while God is not in all their thoughts? Empty shows of pleasure and vain shadows! And even these shadows, these vain flatteries, are ever flying from their embraces; they delude their pursuit in this world and will vanish all at once at the moment of death and leave them in everlasting sorrow. Let the sensualist sport himself in his own deceiving and bless himself in the midst of his madness. Let the rich worldling say, "Soul, take your ease, for your barns and your chests are full." Let the mere philosopher glory that he has found out happiness; let him busy himself in refined subtilties and swell in the pride of his reason. Let all these pretenders to felicity compliment each other, if they please, or call themselves the only happy men.

Yet the meanest and the weakest of all the saints would not make an exchange with them, for the saint is brought near to God. And though his poverty here is never so great and his understanding never so contemptible, yet he knows this great truth well—that to exchange God for the creature would be infinite loss and misery unspeakable. Those who never drew near to God, who never saw God in His works or His Word so as to love Him above all things and partake of His love, must be miserable in spite of all their pretenses. "They that are far from [God] shall perish" (Ps. 73:27).*

---

* Watts, *Works*, 1:125–26.

7

First Degree of Happiness

Happy are those who, though they are sinners by nature, yet are brought so near to God as to be within the sound and call of His grace. In this sense the whole nation of the Jews was a people near to God, for He showed His word to Jacob, His statutes and His judgments to Israel; and on this account they were happy in ancient ages above all kingdoms of the earth (Psalms 147; 148).

Happy those countries where the apostles of Christ planted the gospel and brought grace and salvation near them, though they were before at a dreadful distance from God! Happy Britons in our age! Though we are involved, with the rest of mankind, in the common ruins of our first defection from God, yet we are not left in the darkness of heathenism, on the very confines of hell. But God has exalted us near to heaven and Himself in the ministrations of His word and has led us in a way to His everlasting enjoyment. He has built His sanctuaries among us and established His churches in the midst of us. We are invited to behold the beauty of the Lord, to return to our obedience and His love, and thus be made happy forever.

Blessed are the people who hear and know the joyful sound (Ps. 89:15). But there are degrees of this blessedness, even in the lands that enjoy the gospel. Blessed are those above others who dwell near to the places of public worship; who sit under an enlightening, a powerful and persuasive ministry; who have opportunity to hear the word of God often and who have skill to read it. Blessed are those who are born of religious parents and trained up in the early forms of piety. These are still brought nearer to God; they are nursed, as it were, in His churches and dwell in His courts. And blessed are those who are devoted to the service of the sanctuary, like the priests and Levites of old, who were brought nearest to God among all Israel, for their evil employment, as well as their religious duty, led them continually toward God, heaven, and happiness. But all these glorious privileges are not sufficient to ensure eternal felicity unless we come one step further in approaching to God.*

---

* Watts, *Works*, 1:132.

8

Second Degree of Happiness

Happy are those souls who have been taught to improve their outward advantages of nearness to God so as to obtain reconciliation with Him by the blood of Christ. This is the great end of all the privileges aforementioned, which either Jew or Gentile were partakers of. This was the design of all the approaches that God made toward them. Peace and salvation were preached to those "which were afar off, and to them that were nigh"; and Christ died to "reconcile both unto God"; and that "through him we both have access by one Spirit unto the Father" (Eph. 2:17, 16, 18, respectively). Why are all the alluring glories of the Lord displayed before us in His gospel, but that we might be drawn to love Him? Why are these wondrous manifestations of His grace made to us, but that we might become the objects of His love and taste of His special goodness?

Happy persons who are weary of their old estrangement from God, who have heard and have received the offers of His mercy, who have made their solemn approaches to God by Jesus the Mediator, and who are joined to the Lord in a sweet and everlasting covenant! Happy creatures who behold the beauties of their Maker's face with double pleasure, who love Him with all their souls and begin to taste the love of His heart too. This is a matter of special privilege. Blessed are the men who are thus chosen by divine grace and whom He has caused to approach to Himself by the converting power of His own Spirit! Let them come, let them come, and give up their names to His churches. Let them take up their places and dwell in His courts on earth and thus make a nearer approach to His court of heaven.

O that sinners would once be convinced that there are divine pleasures in religion and joys that the stranger does not interfere with! O that they would be once brought to believe that happiness consists in approaching to God! That they would but give credit to the report of wise and holy men who have lived in humble converse with God many years! What a sacred and superior pleasure it is, above all the joys of sense, to love the great and blessed God and to know that He loves me! To walk all the day in the light of His countenance! To have Him near me as a counselor whose advice I may ask in every difficulty of life! To be ever near Him as my guard and to fly from every danger to the wing of His protection! To have such an almighty Friend with me in sickness and sorrow, in anguish and mortal agonies, and ready to receive my departing spirit into the arms of His love!

O that the formal and nominal Christian who attends divine worship would but once be persuaded that if he come one step nearer to God, his happiness will receive almost an infinite advance! Let the shadows lead him to the substance. Let the image in the glass allure him to converse with the original beauty and the ordinances of grace bring him near

to the God of grace! Let him no longer content himself with pictures of happiness, but give himself up
entirely to the Lord and be made possessor of solid
and substantial felicity. Blessed is the man who has
renounced sin and the world and his heart is over-
powered by divine goodness and brought near to
God in His holy covenant.

Yet there are degrees of blessedness among the
saints on earth. Blessed is every soul whose state and
nature are changed who is not a stranger, but a son.
But more blessed are those sons who are most like
their heavenly Father and keep closest to Him in all
their ways! Blessed are they above others in the holy
family who seldom wander from their God, whose
hearts are always in a heavenly frame, and whose
graces and virtues brighten and improve daily and
make a continual and joyful advance toward the state
of glory!*

* Watts, *Works*, 1:132–33.

9

Third Degree of Happiness

Now let us raise our thoughts and wonder at the blessedness of the saints and angels of the upper world. And blessed are those spirits, whether they belong to bodies or not, whom the Lord has chosen and caused to approach so near Him as to dwell and abide in His higher courts! They are fully satisfied with the goodness of His house, even of His holy temple. The saints are established as pillars in this temple of God and will go no more out. They approach Him in their sublime methods of worship, without the medium of types and ordinances. They see God face-to-face (1 Cor. 13:12). Though ordinances in the church on earth are means of drawing near, yet in that very thing they are also tokens of some degree of estrangement. The saints above are constantly "before the throne" (Rev. 7:15), or night and day serving the Lord, as it is expressed metaphorically, though in truth there is no night there, for they who dwell with God dwell in light everlasting. They approach their Maker in most pleasurable acts of worship, without any interposing cloud to hide His face from them, without clogs and fetters to hold them at a distance, without wanderings, without sins, and without temptations.

O blessed state! O glorious felicity! They behold the beauty of the Lord, transported in divine contemplation, infinitely various and immortal. They feed on His goodness with all the raptures of refined love and are held in long ecstasy under the permanent sensations of the love of God.*

---

* Watts, *Works*, 1:133–34.

THE

W O R K S

OF THE

REVEREND AND LEARNED

ISAAC WATTS, D.D.

CONTAINING, BESIDES HIS

SERMONS, AND ESSAYS ON MISCELLANEOUS SUBJECTS,

SEVERAL ADDITIONAL PIECES,

Selected from his Manuscripts

BY THE

REV. DR. JENNINGS, AND THE REV. DR. DODDRIDGE, IN 1753:

TO WHICH ARE PREFIXED,

MEMOIRS OF THE LIFE OF THE AUTHOR,

COMPILED

BY THE REV. GEORGE BURDER.

IN SIX VOLUMES.

VOL. I.

London:

PRINTED BY AND FOR J. BARFIELD, WARDOUR-STREET,
PRINTER TO HIS ROYAL HIGHNESS THE PRINCE OF WALES.

1810.

The 1810 publication of Watts's works includes his sermons, letters, hymns, poems, philosophical essays, and theological treatises.

10

Fourth Degree of Happiness

A further degree of the blessedness of the man Christ Jesus is that He has a fuller, a richer, and a more transporting sense of the love of God, since God makes nearer approaches to Him and discovers more of His infinite goodness and communicates more of His love. We may venture to say that God loves the human nature of Christ better than He does any other creature, and this human nature has a stronger and more intimate consciousness of the divine love and a sweeter sensation of it than saints or angels can have because of the personal union between the Son of Man and the eternal God. This union, though we know not precisely what it is, yet we know to be sufficient to give Him the name Emmanuel, God with us, which distinguishes it most gloriously from all our unions to God and raises His dignity, His character, and His advantages, even as man, to so sublime a degree above that of all other creatures.

By His exaltation and His dwelling so near to God, His powers are inconceivably enlarged and made capable of taking in higher degrees of felicity. Sights of God stretch the faculties of the soul and enlarge it to receive more of God. This eternal sight has our Redeemer. We see the glory of God chiefly in the face of Christ Jesus, His Son, but He sees the glory of God in His own face and brightness. Christ Himself is the brightness of His Father's glory (Heb. 1:2–3).

As Christ is the medium of our nearness to God, as He is the head of all those who approach to God and the Mediator through whom all approach, so His blessedness is above ours; for in some sense and by way of eminence, He enjoys and feels all that we enjoy and feel, and vastly more too, for He is the medium through which we approach and we enjoy, as well as a person who Himself, and for Himself, approaches and enjoys.

As when a stream of wine or living water is conveyed from the spring by a pipe or channel, the pipe has a tincture of the rich liquor as it flows so, if it is lawful to illustrate things heavenly and divine by things on earth and to bring them down to our ideas by material similitudes; our Lord Jesus, who is authorized to confer life and joy on the saints and through whom all grace, glory, and blessedness are conveyed to them, feels, tastes, and relishes, eminently and in a superior manner, all the joy and the blessedness that He conveys to our souls and all better than we can do, for He is nearer the fountain. He takes a divine and unknown satisfaction in every blessing that He communicates to us. Besides all this, there are some richer streams that terminate and end in Him; the peculiar privileges and pleasures of the good man, while others flow through Him, as the head, down to all His members and give Him the first relish of their sweetness.

When Christ, at the head of all the elect saints, will at the great day draw near to the Father and

say, "Here am I, and the children You have given
Me; those blessed ones whom You have chosen,
that they may approach unto You by Me; I have
often approached You for them, and behold I now
approach with them to the courts of Your upper
house." What manner of joy and glory will this be!
How unspeakably blessed is our Lord Jesus, and we
rejoice with wonder!*

---

* Watts, *Works*, 1:136–37.

11

Fifth Degree of Happiness

Our admiration may be raised yet higher if we make one excursion beyond all created nature and lift our thoughts upward to the blessedness of the three glorious persons in the Trinity. All their infinite and unknown pleasures are derived from their ineffable union and communion in one Godhead, their inconceivable nearness to each other in the very center and spring of all felicity. They are inseparably and intimately one with God; they are eternally one God and therefore eternally blessed. "For there are three that bear record in heaven, the Father, the Word, and the Holy Ghost: and these three are one" (1 John 5:7). I believe this text to be authentic and divine, and that on just reasons, notwithstanding all the cavils and criticisms that have endeavored to blot it out of the Bible. Nor is their blessedness or their nearness a dull, inactive state. Knowledge and mutual love make up their heaven as far as mortals dare conceive of it and as far as we have leave to speak of God after the manner of men.

An eternal, blissful contemplation of all the infinite beauties, powers, and properties of Godhead and of all the operations of these powers in an inconceivable variety among creatures is the glorious employment of God. His own knowledge of infinite truths, whether wrapped up in His own nature or unfolded and displayed in His works, is a pleasure becoming the Deity, and each sacred person possesses this unknown pleasure.

But God's contemplation, or knowledge, of Himself is not His only pleasure, "for God is love" (1 John 4:8). He has an infinite propensity toward Himself and an inconceivable complacence in His own powers and perfections, as well as in all the outgoings of them toward created natures. His love being most wise and perfect must exert itself toward the most perfect object and the chief good, and in a degree answerable to its goodness too. Therefore He can love nothing in the same degree with Himself because He can find no equal good.

As the blessed Three have an unknown communion in the Godhead, or divine nature, so they must have an unspeakable nearness to one another's persons, an inconceivable inbeing and indwelling in each other. "I am in the Father, and the Father [is] in me" (John 14:10). Each is near to the other two divine subsistences, and this mutual nearness must be attended with delight and felicity unknown to all but the blessed Three who enjoy it. O glorious and divine communion! The Father forever near to His own image, the Son, and herein blessed! The Son never divided from the embraces of the Father and therefore happy! The Spirit everlastingly near them both, and therefore He is the ever-blessed Spirit! And all these united in one Godhead and therefore infinitely and forever blessed!*

---

* Watts, *Works*, 1:137–38.

SECTION TWO

The Foundation of Piety

——◦——

12

The Ruin of Man

As Adam produced his offspring like himself, destitute of the image of God or defiled with sinful inclinations, so he also produced them destitute of the favor of God, or in a state of disfavor with their Maker, because they were under the same sentence of condemnation, misery, and death, together with himself. As I have proved this before by showing that pains and agonies and often death itself, which is the appointed punishment of sin, seizes on children immediately from their birth, before they are capable of committing actual sin, so there are some Scripture verses that lead us into the same sentiment, as Job 14:1: "Man that is born of a woman is of few days and full of trouble." That is, his short life and his troubles or miseries proceed from his very birth, or his propagation from his sinful and mortal parents. Otherwise God would not have appointed His noblest creature in this world to have been born to trouble. Yet this is the case: "Man is born unto trouble, as the sparks fly upward" (Job 5:7)—that is, naturally, for it is owing to his birth and his natural derivation from a sinful stock. We are a miserable race of beings, springing from a corrupted and dying root, prone to sin, and liable to sorrows and sufferings.

Yet let it be observed here concerning one man, even Jesus Christ, that though He is the son of Adam in a large sense, yet by this propagation He does not fall under that guilt and condemnation or that degeneracy of nature and those sinful propensities that are conveyed to the rest of Adam's posterity. And the reason is plain—namely, because He was not the son of Adam by natural generation or by propagation but by a miraculous operation of God and His Spirit, taking part of the body, or flesh and blood, of the virgin Mary and making a man child of it (Luke 1:34–35). And thus Christ had no original sin inherent or even imputed by the same constitution and on the same account as other children have, but was perfectly innocent. And consequently, He had not been exposed to suffer sickness and death, which other children are exposed to, nor subject to any of our sorrows if He had not been a voluntary undertaker to rescue and redeem fallen man by having all our sins imputed to Him and suffered in our stead.*

---

* Watts, *Works*, 6:120.

13

Original Sin, or, the
First and Second Adam

Backward with humble shame we look
On our original;
How is our nature dash'd and broke
In our first father's fall!

To all that's good-averse and blind,
But prone to all that's ill:
What dreadful darkness veils our mind!
How obstinate our will.

Conceiv'd in sin (O wretched state!)
Before we draw our breath,
The first young pulse begins to beat
Iniquity and death.

How strong in our degenerate blood
The old corruption reigns,
And mingling with the crooked flood,
Wanders thro' all our veins!

Wild and unwholesome as the root
Will all the branches be;
How can we hope for living fruit
From such a deadly tree?

What mortal power from things unclean
Can pure productions bring?
Who can command a vital stream
From an infected spring?

Yet, mighty God, Thy wondrous love
Can make our nature clean,
While Christ and grace prevail above
The tempter, death, and sin.

The second Adam shall restore
The ruins of the first,
Hosanna to that sovereign power
That new creates our dust.*

---

* Watts, *Works*, 4:269–70.

HYMNS

AND

Spiritual Songs.

In Three BOOKS.

I. Collected from the Scriptures.
II. Compos'd on Divine Subjects.
III. Prepared for the Lord's Supper.

With an ESSAY

Towards the Improvement of Christian Psalmody, by the Use of Evangelical Hymns in Worship, as well as the Psalms of *David*.

By *I. WATTS.*

And they sung a new Song, saying, Thou art worthy, &c. for thou waft slain and haft redeemed us, &c. Rev. 5. 9.
Soliti essent *(i. e. Christiani)* convenire, carmenque Christo quasi Deo dicere. *Plinius in Epist.*

LONDON,

Printed by *J. Humfreys,* for *John Lawrence,*
at the Angel in the *Poultrey.* 1707.

A first edition of Watts's *Hymns and Spiritual Songs* originally published in 1707

14

Natural Death

Natural death, or the death of the body, is one thing plainly designed in the first threatening, beyond all controversy. The natural life of the sinner is forfeited to Him who gave it when he has once broken his allegiance to his Creator and supreme Lord. That this is the first and most obvious idea of the punishment threatened may be plainly proved because this is the universal, common, and literal meaning of the word *death* in all human languages.

This is also the very sense of the same writer, Moses, when he uses the same words in all other parts of his writings—namely, "You will surely die"; or, "In dying you will die." In those places it means evidently temporal death, as might be proved easily if we consult all those places.

And let it be observed that in those early ages, the future and invisible world being very little brought into view, the word *death* might naturally include in it the forfeiture of all being and all comforts whatsoever since it evidently means the loss and forfeiture of all visible being, life, and comforts, for all these appear to vanish at death.

Besides, this death of the body was positively foretold to Adam and was the sentence pronounced on him when he had actually sinned: "Dust thou art, and unto dust shalt thou return" (Gen. 3:19). And accordingly we find that when Adam is said to beget a son in his own likeness—that is, in his own mortal likeness, in contradistinction to the glorious and immortal likeness of God in which, the foregoing verses tell us, he was first made (Gen. 5:1–3)—then the Scripture goes on to prove it by showing how this death was executed. A plain account follows of the natural death of Adam and a long succession of the deaths of his posterity, as being made mortal in the image of Adam, their natural head.

And as has been shown before that not only life but health and ease and the comforts of life, being the free gifts of God our Creator, they are all forfeited by the offense of His creature against Him. And all the pains and sorrows and sicknesses of this life, which by degrees tend to wear out nature and to bring man down to the dust, may be justly supposed to be implied in his threatening of death.

And as this natural death of the body is plainly implied in the first threatening, as a penalty for sin to come upon Adam and his posterity, so not only all the books of Moses but perhaps all the Old Testament do scarce afford us any instances wherein the word *death*, properly and without a figure, is taken to signify anything else plainly but the sorrows and miseries of this life and the final deprivation of life itself; though, in the first threatening, tacitly, it may include the forfeiture of everything God had before given, so far as God pleased to resume it.*

---

* Watts, *Works*, 6:136–37.

15

———— ⊶ ⊷ ————

Spiritual Death

The next thing our divines have usually included in the word *dying* is spiritual death, which has been generally extended to signify the anguish of a guilty conscience, the loss of the divine image in holiness with the loss of the divine favor, and the infliction of new sorrows on the soul. Let us consider each of these apart and see how far they may be included in the first threatening.

First, the anguish of conscience can never belong to any but the personal transgressor himself because it consists in the uneasy and painful reflections of the mind of him who has sinned, charging himself with his own act of folly and disobedience. This is the natural effect, or consequent, of personal sin and not so properly the threatened penalty of the law. This anguish does not come upon the offspring of Adam by imputation on account of the first sin, for it can never be imputed to another person by any representation or suretyship. Nor can it ever be conveyed or transmitted by any natural propagation or descent, for, in the nature of things, anguish of conscience can only belong to the very person who is conscious of his own actual folly and rebellion, which another person can never be conscious of. This anguish of conscience cannot be communicated to the offspring of Adam on account of Adam's original sin alone. Rather, when a person becomes a personal sinner, they feel this anguish of conscience also arising from their own actual transgressions as the natural consequence of a guilty mind.

Second, the loss of the image of God in holiness is another thing contained in spiritual death, and in the New Testament, this is termed by St. Paul a death "in trespasses and sins" (Eph. 2:1). It consists in the corruption of human nature and a bias or propensity toward evil. But this cannot be so properly threatened as the penalty of the law to be inflicted for the sin of Adam, for the holy and righteous God cannot be the author of sin in His creatures. He cannot infuse sin into the nature of man, or take away his virtues by any divine act, or make him vicious as a natural effect or consequent of man's first sin.

Third, the soul's loss of the favor of God is another part of spiritual death. The loss of the manifestations of God's love or friendly converse with Him and any peculiar instances of His grace may be included in the words *spiritual death*. "He that loveth not his brother abideth in death" (1 John 3:14). And perhaps this may be also included in that scriptural expression because those who are dead in trespasses and sins are said to be "children of wrath" (Eph. 2:1–3), or obnoxious to the divine anger.*

---

* Watts, *Works*, 6:137–38.

16

Eternal Death

Eternal death consists in the misery of both soul and body in the invisible world and in a future state. Thus it is generally explained by our writers and has been often said to be included in the penalty due to the first sin. Let us here inquire into it.

First, let us consider it as it relates to the soul of man. The soul is an immaterial and thinking being, and it has in itself no natural principles of dissolution; therefore, as far as we can judge, it must be immortal in its own nature. But who can say whether the word *death* might not be fairly construed to extend to the utter destruction of the life of the soul as well as of the body if God the righteous governor should please to seize the forfeiture? For man by sin had forfeited all that God had given him—that is, the life and existence of his soul as well as his body. All is forfeited by sin into the hands of God. And why might not the threatening declare the right that even a God of goodness had to resume all back again and utterly destroy and annihilate His creatures forever?

Second, the other part of eternal death, or eternal misery, consists in the raising up of the body again from the dead and rejoining it to the soul in order to be made eternally miserable together with the soul, or rather to be an everlasting instrument of the soul's misery and torment.

So that as the gospel or covenant of grace has provided hope and salvation by Jesus the Mediator for all who would accept it, whether under the patriarchal, Jewish, or Christian dispensation, so those who continue impenitent and will not return to God according to this new covenant are exposed to double punishment under the government of the Mediator. And He will raise them from the dead to receive the reward of their obstinacy and impenitence, their violation of the law of God, and their neglect of all the means and hopes of grace.*

---

* Watts, *Works*, 6:139–40.

John Locke (1632–1704)

Watts often interacted in his own writings with this eighteenth-century Enlightenment philosopher. Contrary to Locke, Watts believed that because of original sin, reason alone could not lead to repentance and faith.

17

The Recovery of Man

The effects of the fall, or sin of man, under which
these favorites, or elect of God, continue are such
as these: namely, God suffers them to come into
the world with a sinful nature, uncured, unsanct-
fied, and to continue under some evil operations
and influences of this sinful nature all their lives,
that they might conflict with it and overcome it by
His assistances. He appoints them also to continue
during all this mortal life subject to many pains,
afflictions, sorrows, and miseries for wise ends and
purposes in His economy of grace; and at last that
their bodies should die and turn to dust, according to
the original threatening of death.

The deliverance, or salvation, that God provided
for them was that they should be restored to the favor
and image of God again and brought at last to eternal life and happiness in this manner: namely, that
they should have a most lively sense or perception of
their own guilt and misery and of the hope of mercy,
so far as to encourage their repentance for past sins
and their return to God by a new obedience.

And so far as the gospel of Christ came within
their notice, they should learn the saving methods
of grace by Christ Jesus. And to this end, all these
things should be set before their minds by divine

impressions on their understanding, as well as by
the Word. This is called *enlightening their minds* in the
knowledge of their sin and misery and of the way of
salvation by Christ.

And yet further, God provided salvation so
that they should have their sinful natures in some
measure sanctified, or made holy, here on earth by
a great change wrought on them by God's Holy
Spirit, which is called *regeneration* or *being born again*;
that they should be enabled by the Spirit of God to
comply with all the proposals or necessary terms of
this covenant of grace or salvation, which should
be appointed them by God Himself, as governor of
the world, or by Jesus Christ His Son, as His great
vicegerent and Lord of all.

God also provided salvation so that their sins
should be pardoned, both original and actual, so far
as never to be shut out of the favor of God and the
promise of eternal life on account of them. Yet that
they should sustain such sorrows and sufferings in
their way to eternal happiness as might teach them
the evil nature and the bitter fruits of sin and by
degrees wean them from it. That they should have
many assistances, reliefs, and comforts under the
difficulties and trials, sorrows and miseries that they
sustain in this life.

Finally, He provided salvation so that their souls
should be received into a holy and peaceful state
in the presence of Christ in heaven at the death of
their bodies. And that their bodies should be raised
again at the last day and be rejoined to their souls,
at which time they should be publicly acquitted and

acknowledged as the sons of God and be freed from all the unhappy effects and penalties of the fall of Adam and be thenceforth made forever happy in the presence of God.*

* Watts, *Works*, 6:143–44.

18

Christ's Mediation

Have you heard, O my soul, have you learned the glorious discoveries that God has made of Himself to fallen creatures, and does not your heart rejoice within you at the sound of such a doctrine and such a salvation? Has the blessed God revealed Himself to you in His beloved Son and by His Holy Spirit? And does He invite you to approach Him as a Father by such a divine Mediator and such a divine Sanctifier? O let all the powers of your nature submit with joy to all the discoveries of such a grace! Go, humble yourself before an offended God who is willing to become a Father and a Friend. Go in the name of Jesus, the great Mediator, and make your approaches to the throne. Seek the influences of the Holy Spirit to enlighten your dark understanding, to conquer the obstinacy of your will, and subdue all your affections to a sincere compliance with this method of divine love. And let the constraining force of this sweet doctrine unite your heart to all your fellow Christians, who sincerely worship the same God, who seek for acceptance through the blood of the same Mediator, and who depend on the aids of the same Spirit.

Happy day when faith and holiness and love will be found shining and reigning among all who profess the religion of Christ! O when will that promised hour appear, that the Lord Jehovah "shall be king over all the earth," and there "shall…be one LORD, and his name one" (Zech. 14:9)? Blessed Jesus, have You by Your death "broken down the middle wall of partition" that stood between the Jews and the Gentiles? Have You reconciled "both unto God in one body by the cross, having slain the enmity thereby" (Eph. 2:14, 16)?

What wretched creatures are we then to build up new walls of partition ourselves by inventing and imposing new forms of faith and worship that Your Word has not taught us and for which it has given us no foundation! What wretched creatures are we to raise up so many new enmities in the Christian church and support them with fierce and implacable zeal and fury! This is to walk as enemies, even to the cross of Christ, and contrary to the compassionate designs of a dying Savior. One would think that the blood of the Son of God crucified should teach us kinder lessons.

O when will all these enmities be abolished by the overpowering influence of the Spirit of light and love? When will these unhappy walls of partition be broken down, and the whole flock of Christ become one blessed fold under Jesus, the universal Shepherd? When will we arrive at the perfect unity of the faith and maintain the unity of the Spirit in the bond of love (Eph. 4:13, 3, respectively)? When will the glory and beauty of the primitive church be restored, where the "multitude of them that believed were of one heart and of one soul" (Acts 4:32), united in one faith and hope by the almighty influences of one Spirit?

Come, blessed Redeemer, come and accomplish Your own gracious words of promise. Let there be one fold and one Shepherd, and let Your blood and Your Spirit, by which we have access to one God, even the Father, cement all our hearts to each other in such a union as will never be dissolved. Then will we join with all the creation in one eternal song, even the song that Your Word has taught us: "Blessing, and honour, and glory, and power, be unto him that sitteth upon the throne, and unto the Lamb for ever and ever" (Rev. 5:13). Amen.[*]

---

[*] Watts, *Works*, 1:496–97.

19

Access to the Throne of Grace
by a Mediator

Come let us lift our joyful eyes
Up to the courts above,
And smile to see our Father there
Upon a throne of love.

Once 'twas a seat of dreadful wrath,
And shot devouring flame;
Our God appear'd consuming fire,
And vengeance was His name.

Rich were the drops of Jesus's blood
That calm'd His frowning face,
That sprinkled o'er the flashing throne,
And quench'd it into grace.

Now we may bow before His feet,
And venture near the Lord;
No fiery cherub guards His seat,
Nor double flaming sword.

The peaceful gates of heavenly bliss
Are open'd by the Son;
High let us raise our notes of praise,
And reach the almighty throne.

To Thee ten thousand thanks we bring,
Great Advocate on high,
And glory to th' Eternal King,
That lays His fury by.[*]

---

[*] Watts, *Works*, 4:329.

Elizabeth Singer Rowe (1674–1737)

Watts was close friends with the hymn writer and even proposed marriage to her at one point, but he was turned down. Watts edited and published her work *Devout Exercises of the Heart* (1737).

20

Christ's Atonement

Inquire now, O my soul, do you believe in Christ? Have you seen your heavy guilt and your danger of eternal death? Have you been weary and heavy laden with a sense of your past iniquities? Have you been pained at heart under the present power of indwelling sin? And have you fled for refuge to the hope set before you in the gospel? Have you joyfully received Jesus the Savior by faith in His blood? By a living and active faith? Have you committed yourself to Him to be delivered from the reign of sin, as well as from the condemnation of it? Then you may join with the blessed apostle and speak in the language of faith, He "loved me, and gave himself for me" (Gal. 2:20).

Let me meditate again on the sorrows and agonies of my dear, my adored Redeemer. Infinite agonies and sorrows beyond all the powers of language! Is my heart made of stone, that it can hear such a history and not melt within me? Have I no tender part within me to bleed at the rehearsal of such anguish and such love? Blessed Jesus, smite the rock of my heart, and let it pour out new streams of repentance and affectionate gratitude! I was dead, and the Son of God gave Himself up to death in order to raise me to life again. I was a traitor and an enemy, and He has sustained the arrows of the Almighty to reconcile me to His Father and turn away His infinite indignation. My great High Priest has offered up Himself a bloody sacrifice for me, that my guilt might be forgiven and canceled forever.

Think, O my soul, study, contrive, speak. What will you render to the Lord for such astonishing condescension and such unexampled grace? How will you show the inestimable value of His atonement? What does He require of you but to keep those garments clean that He has washed in so rich a fountain as His own blood? And will I ever willfully indulge the practice of sin again and return to my old defilements? Will I ever consent to break the law of my God? Have I not seen the dreadful nature and dismal effects of it in the agonies and death of my dearest Lord? What will I do that I may never sin more? Lord, I cannot preserve myself from the fatal infection while I dwell in a world where sin reigns all around me, in a world that lies in wickedness, and while I am so nearly allied to flesh and blood; where folly, vice, and sin run through every vein to my heart. Jesus, I commit myself afresh to Your care. You will save the soul that You have purchased at so dear a rate; You will accept and save a returning penitent. Here I devote my life, myself, my flesh and spirit, and all my powers to Your obedience and the purposes of Your glory forever and ever. My soul looks up to You with an eye of humble confidence, and my faith and hope rest on Your everlasting love. Amen.*

---

* Watts, *Works*, 1:369–70.

21

The Use of the Atonement

Let us use this atonement of Christ as our constant way of access to God in all our prayers. This is the only safe method of address to the mercy seat. It is ordained for this very purpose, to help a sinner near to God. "Having therefore, brethren, boldness to come into the holiest by the blood of Jesus…and having an high priest over the house of God; let us draw near with a true heart" (Heb. 10:19, 21–22). He is ascended to heaven before us; He is entered within the veil in virtue of His sacrifice. He has reserved acceptance for our persons before the throne and a favorable audience for all our prayers. Whatever we ask of the Father, we must ask it in His name, and especially in the name and virtue of His great atonement. All the blessings that God has to bestow are purchased by His sufferings.

Reflection: "Remember, O my soul, and be humble; remember you cannot be a welcome guest even at the throne of grace unless you are sprinkled with the blood of Jesus. The God whom you have offended is a great God and terrible; a God of holiness, like a devouring fire; a God of awful majesty and severe justice, who will by no means clear the guilty without some recompense for His broken law. Dare not approach Him, therefore, but under the protection of the blood of His Son. Christ is set forth as our propitiation through faith in His blood. If you bring the atonement of Christ in the hand of your faith, you will find sweet and easy access. And when you are filled with inward sorrows, you may pour them all out and spread your complaints and your burdens before the eyes of your God, with inward consolation and hope.

"Lord, I have sinned, but Your Son has suffered. I come to the throne of grace in His name. My offenses cry for vengeance, but the blood of Jesus speaks better things and cries louder for peace and pardon. Let the voice of that blood which has made full satisfaction for the vilest sins prevail over all my unworthiness. Let the Lamb who is in the midst of the throne be honored this day by introducing a guilty creature, with all his complaints and sorrows, into Your awful presence and Your divine favor. Let me obtain grace in the hour of my distress and necessity. And O that I may find such success and such ease of soul in drawing near to God by the blood of Christ, that on all occasions I may run to this refuge and maintain humble and constant communion with God my Father in this new and living way of access. May this earthly and foolish spirit of mine never be such a stranger as it has been at the mercy seat since the door of approach is always open since I have so glorious an introducer."*

---

* Watts, *Works*, 1:388.

22

Death, the Last Enemy

Death is the last enemy that the saints have to
grapple with in this world. The three great adversaries of a Christian are the flesh, the world, and the
devil, and they assault him often in this life. Death
comes behind and brings up the rear; the saint
combats with this enemy and finishes all the war.
Every believer has listed himself under the banner
of Christ, who is the Captain of his salvation. When
he first gives himself up to the Lord, he renounces
everything that is inconsistent with his faith and
hope, abandons his former slavery, undertakes the
spiritual warfare, and enters the field of battle. It
is a necessary character of the followers of Christ
that they fight with the flesh, subdue corrupt nature,
suppress their irregular appetites, give daily wounds
to the body of sin (Rom. 8:13; Col. 3:5). They fight
against this world; they refuse to comply with the
temptations of it when it would allure them astray
from the path of duty; they defy its frowns and discouragements and break through all its oppositions
in their way to heaven (James 4:4). They resist Satan
when he tempts them to sin and vanquish him by
"the sword of the Spirit, which is the word of God"
(Eph. 6:11–12, 17). And when he accuses them
and attempts to bring terror into their souls, they

overcome him and cast him down by the blood of the Lamb (Rev. 12:10–11). They are made conquerors over these adversaries in the strength of Christ. Now the pangs of death are the last troublers of their peace; death is the last enemy that attacks them, and some have very terrible conflicts with it.

Death may be called the last enemy because it is not utterly destroyed till the resurrection, till Christ has done all His work on earth, till He has subdued all His other adversaries and made use of death as His slave to destroy many of them. It is in this sense especially that the words of my text, 1 Corinthians 15:24–26, are written by St. Paul: "Then cometh the end, when he shall have delivered up the kingdom to God, even the Father; when he shall have put down all rule and all authority and power. For he must reign, till he hath put all enemies under his feet. The last enemy that shall be destroyed is death."

With regard to each particular Christian, all other enemies are destroyed when he dies, for where he goes they cannot come. He puts off the body of flesh and of sin together; he leaves every corruption behind him when he ascends to the company of the spirits of the just made perfect. The smiles and the frowns of this vain and vexing world are too far off to influence the inhabitants of heaven; and Satan, the tempter and accuser, is forever forbid entrance at the gates of that holy city. But death holds one part of the saint in his prison, the grave. And though the departed soul has overcome the terrors of this enemy and triumphs in this expression, "O death, where is thy sting?" yet the body is confined as a prisoner under his power. But the hour is coming when those who are dead will hear the voice of the Son of God and live. All the prisons of the saints will be broken to pieces and burned up, and the keeper destroyed forever.[*]

---

[*] Watts, *Works*, 2:13–14.

23

Perfection of Heaven

Temptation and sin have no place in those happy regions. These are the evils that belong to earth and hell; but within the gates of heaven, nothing must enter that tempts, nothing that defiles (Rev. 21:27). It is the mixture of sinful thoughts and idle words, sinful actions and irregular affections, that makes our state of holiness so imperfect here below. We groan within ourselves, being burdened; we would be rid of these criminal weaknesses, these guilty attendants of our lives. But the spirits above are under a sweet necessity of being forever holy; their natures have put on perfection. The image of God is so far completed in them that nothing contrary to the divine nature remains in all their frame, for they see God in all the fairest beauties of His holiness, and they adore and love. They behold Him without a veil and "are changed into the same image from glory to glory" (2 Cor. 3:18). If these words are applicable to the state of grace, much more to that of glory. They see Christ as He is, and they are made completely like Him (1 John 3:2).

As their love to God is perfect, so is their love to all their fellow saints. We try to love our fellow creatures and fellow Christians here on earth, but we have so many corrupt passions of our own, and so many infirmities and imperfections belong to our neighbors also, that mutual love is very imperfect. "Love is the fulfilling of the law" (Rom. 13:10). But we will never fulfill that law perfectly till we are joined to the spirits of the just in glory, where there is no inhabitant without the flame of sacred love, no single spirit unlovely or unbeloved.

In those happy mansions there is no envy raised by the perfections or the honors of our neighbor spirits; no detracting thought is known there; no reproachful word is heard in that country, and perhaps no word of reproach is to be found in the whole heavenly language. Malice and slander and the very names of infamy are unknown in those regions, and wrath and strife are eternal strangers. No divided opinions, no party quarrels, no seeds of discord are sown in heaven. Our little angry bickerings and contentions have no place there, and the noise of war and controversy ceases forever. There are no offenses given, and none are taken in that world of love. Neither injury nor resentment is ever known or practiced there, those bitter and fatal springs of revenge and blood. Universal benevolence runs through the whole kingdom. Each spirit wishes well to his neighbor as to himself, and till we arrive there, we will never be made perfect in love nor will we see the blessed characters of it described in the Scriptures fully copied out in living examples.

In that holy world dwells God Himself, who is original love; there resides our Lord Jesus Christ, who is love incarnate. And from that sacred Head flows an eternal stream of love through every member and blesses all the inhabitants of that land with its divine refreshments. Holiness is perfect among the spirits of the just because love is perfect there.[*]

---

[*] Watts, *Works*, 2:28–29.

John Milton (1608–1674)

The poet was a favorite of Watts. He often quoted from Milton's famous work *Paradise Lost*.

Picture courtesy of Llyfrgell Genedlaethol Cymru—
The National Library of Wales

24

Death a Blessing to the Saints

Do flesh and nature dread to die?
And timorous thoughts our minds enslave?
But grace can raise our hopes on high,
And quell the terrors of the grave.

What! Shall we run to gain the crown,
Yet grieve to think the goal so near?
Afraid to have our labors done,
And finish this important war?

Do we not dwell in clouds below,
And little know the God we love?
Why should we like this twilight so,
When 'tis all noon in worlds above?

There shall we see Him face-to-face,
There shall we know the great unknown:
And Jesus, with His glorious grace,
Shines in full light amidst the throne.

When we put off this fleshly load,
We're from a thousand mischiefs free,
For ever present with our God,
Where we have long'd and wish'd to be.

No more shall pride or passion rise,
Or envy fret, or malice roar,
Or sorrow mourn with downcast eyes,
And sin defile our souls no more.

'Tis best, 'tis infinitely best,
To go where tempters cannot come,
Where saints and angels ever blest,
Dwell and enjoy their heavenly home.

O for a visit from my God,
To drive my fears of death away,
And help me thro' this darksome road,
To realms of everlasting day!*

* Watts, *Works*, 1:477.

25

Death and Heaven

ODE I
*The Spirit's Farewell to the Body after
Long Sickness*

I.

How am I held a prisoner now,
Far from my God! This mortal chain
Binds me to sorrow. All below
Is short-liv'd ease or tiresome pain.

II.

When shall that wondrous hour appear,
Which frees me from this dark abode,
To live at large in regions, where
Nor cloud nor veil shall hide my God?

III.

Farewell this flesh, these ears, these eyes,
These snares and fetters of the mind;
My God, nor let this frame arise
Till every dust be well refin'd.

IV.

Jesus, who mak'st our natures whole,
Mold me a body like Thy own:
Then shall it better serve my soul
In works of praise and worlds unknown.

ODE II

The Departing Moment; or, Absent from the Body

I.

Absent from flesh! O blissful thought!
What unknown joys this moment brings!
Freed from the mischiefs sin hath wrought,
From pains and tears and all their springs.

II.

Absent from flesh! Illustrious day!
Surprising scene! Triumphant stroke,
That rends the prison of my clay,
And I can feel my fetters broke!

III.

Absent from flesh! Then rise, my soul,
Where feet or wings could never climb,
Beyond the heav'ns where planets roll,
Measuring the cares and joys of time.

IV.

I go where God and glory shine:
His presence makes eternal day.
My all that's mortal I resign,
For Uriel waits and points my way.

ODE III

Entrance into Paradise; or, Present with the Lord

I.

And is this heav'n? And am I there?
How short the road! How swift the flight!
I am all life, all eye, all ear;
Jesus is here—my soul's delight.

II.

Is this the heav'nly Friend who hung
In blood and anguish on the tree,
Whom Paul proclaim'd, whom David sung,
Who died for them, who died for me?

III.

How fair Thou offspring of my God!
Thou firstborn image of His face!
Thy death procur'd this blest abode,
Thy vital beams adorn the place.

IV.

Lo, He presents me at the throne
All spotless; there the Godhead reigns
Sublime and peaceful thro' the Son
Awake, my voice, in heav'nly strains.

ODE IV

The Sight of God in Heaven

I.

Creator God, eternal light,
Fountain of good, tremendous power,
Ocean of wonders, blissful sight!
Beauty and love unknown before!

II.

Thy grace, Thy nature, all unknown
In yon dark region whence I came;
Where languid glimpses from Thy throne
And feeble whispers teach Thy name.

III.

I'm in a world where all is new;
Myself, my God; O blest amaze!
Not my best hopes or wishes knew
To form a shadow of this grace.

IV.

Fix'd on my God, my heart, adore:
My restless thoughts, forbear to rove:
Ye meaner passions, stir no more;
But all my powers be joy and love.[*]

---

[*] Watts, *Works*, 1:593.

Richard Baxter (1615–1691)

The Puritan pastor and theologian influenced Watts, who agreed with and passed along many of Baxter's theological convictions.

Picture courtesy of Llyfrgell Genedlaethol Cymru—
The National Library of Wales

26

Preparation for Heaven

Awake, awake, O impenitent sinners, who are as yet unprepared for the business and blessedness of the heavenly state; awake and exert your souls in warmest reflections on matters of infinite importance.

First, think with yourselves how much the great God has done toward the preparation of sinful men for this heaven; think seriously of His long-suffering goodness and His sparing mercy, which should have led you long ago to a melting sense of your own folly and brought you back to Him by humble repentance. For what reason were His patience and His long-suffering exercised toward you if not for this very purpose (Rom. 2:4)? Think of the blessings of nature with which He has surrounded you and the comforts of this life wherewith He has furnished you in order to allure your thoughts toward Him who is the spring of all goodness and to raise your desires toward Him. It is He who invites you, who will be the everlasting portion and happiness of His people, and in whose favor consist life and felicity. Dare not any longer neglect your preparation for this happiness, which consists in the enjoyment of God, lest you should be cut off before you are prepared.

Second, consider again what Jesus, the Son of God, has done and suffered, and consider what

He is yet doing toward the preparation of souls for heaven. He came down to our world to undertake the glorious and dreadful work of the redemption of sinners from the curse of the law and the terrors of hell and to procure a heaven for every rebellious creature who would return to God his Father. Think of the agonies of His death with which He purchased mansions of glory for those who receive His grace in His own appointed methods, those who are willing to have their hearts and minds formed into a suitable frame to receive this felicity. Remember that He is risen from the dead; He is ascended to prepare a place in glory for those who are willing to follow Him through the paths of holiness. Hearken to the many kind invitations and allurements of His gospel, which calls to the worst of sinners to return and live, and entreats and exhorts those who are in the ends of the earth and on the borders of hell to look to Him that they may be saved (Isa. 45:22). Take heed that you suffer not these seasons of His inviting love to slide away and vanish unimproved; take heed how you rebel against the language of the grace of His gospel and thereby prepare yourselves for double and everlasting destruction.

Third, think again what blessed assistances He has proposed to those who are desirous to be trained up for heaven. How many thousand souls as carnal, as sensual, and as criminal as yours is have been recovered by the word of His gospel and the influences of His Spirit to a new nature and life of holiness? How many are there who from children of wrath have become the sons and daughters of the Most High God, heirs of this blessedness, and prepared for the enjoyment of it? O take heed that you resist not His grace or rebel against the kind and sacred motions of the blessed Spirit within you, when His very office and business is to change your sinful natures and to prepare you for the regions of eternal holiness and peace.*

* Watts, *Works*, 2:212–13.

The Cultivation of Piety

27

Holy Wonder

If the soul is warmed with divine love, the various discoveries that God makes of Himself to us will not only be matter of frequent contemplation but of pleasing wonder. Admiration or wonder is a noble passion, arising from the view of something that is new and strange or on the notice of some rare and uncommon object. Now when so glorious and transcendent a being as the great and blessed God becomes the object of our notice and our love, with what pleasure do we survey His glories, which are so rare, so uncommon, that there are none to compare with them? We will meditate on the surprising discoveries that He has made of Himself till we find new matter of holy admiration in all of them. Sincere and fervent love is ever finding some new beauties and wonders in the person so much beloved.

There is sufficient matter in God for the pleasurable and everlasting entertainment of this holy passion. He is an immense ocean of glories and wonders. There is nothing in God but what would be marvelous and astonishing to us if we had our eyes divinely enlightened and our hearts fired with divine love. Every creature has something in it that surpasses our knowledge and commands our admiration. But what are all these in comparison to God, the all-wise and almighty Artificer, who made them all by His wisdom and the breath of His mouth? The soul who loves God is ready to see and take notice of God in everything. He walks through the fields; he observes the wonders of divine workmanship in every different tree on his right hand and on his left, in the herbs and flowers that he treads with his feet, in the rich diversity of shapes and colors and ornaments of nature. He beholds and admires his God in them all. He sees the birds in their airy flight or perched on the branches and sending forth their various melody. He observes the grazing flocks and the larger cattle in their different forms and manners of life. He looks down on little insects and takes notice of their vigorous and busy life and motions, their shining bodies, and their golden or painted wings. He beholds and he admires his God in them all. In the least things of nature, he can read the greatness of God, and it is what of God he finds in the creature that renders creatures more delightful to him. Creatures are but his steps to help him rise toward God.

I might add, after all, there is yet still another world of wonders to employ the lover of God, and that is the person of His Son, Jesus Christ our Savior. There God discovers Himself in His fullest grace and wisdom, in His highest power and perfection. The attributes of the Father shine transcendently glorious in His Son and become the object of love and wonder to men and angels. He is the fairest "image of the invisible God, the firstborn of every creature" (Col. 1:15). He is "the brightness of [the Father's] glory, and the express image of his person" (Heb. 1:3).

All the marvelous things that God the Father ever wrought—it was in and by His Son. Did He create all things out of nothing? It was by Jesus Christ (Eph. 3:9). Does He govern the world with amazing wisdom? It is by making His Son Jesus the governor and Lord of all things. Does He redeem and save guilty sinners from everlasting misery? These wonders of mercy are transacted by the cradle and the cross of Jesus; by the death and the life of Christ; by the sorrows, the sufferings, and the victories of the Son of God. His name is called Wonderful (Isa. 9:6), for He who is the child born is also the mighty God. The infant of days is the everlasting Father, the first and the last, the beginning and the end of all things. What sublime and sacred raptures of love and wonder join together when a devout Christian contemplates his God in His nature, in His providences, in all His works, in the pages of His Holy Book, and in the face of His Son, the blessed Jesus!*

---

* Watts, *Works*, 2:643–45.

John Owen (1616–1683)

This Puritan is often cited by Watts. Watts pastored the same church (Mark Lane Independent Chapel) that Owen had formerly pastored.

Picture courtesy of Llyfrgell Genedlaethol Cymru—
The National Library of Wales

28

The Invaluable Regulator

If divine love is so sovereign and ruling an affection, then the best and noblest method for governing all the passions is to get the love of God rooted in the heart and to see that it maintain its supreme dominion there. What uneasy creatures are we made by our various passions! How often do they disquiet and torment the soul! How headstrong is their violence, like a horse unbroken and untamed! How sudden are their starts! Their motions how wild and various! And how unruly are their efforts! Now, if one had but one sovereign bridle that could reach and manage them all, one golden rein that would hold in all their unruly motions and would also excite and guide them at pleasure, what an invaluable instrument would this be to mortals! Surely such an instrument is the love of God, such an invaluable regulator of all the passionate powers, and it will have this effect where it is strong and supreme, as it ought to be.

You who are daily disturbed and led astray by rising passions of various kinds, come to the lectures of the gospel, come to the doctrine of the blessed Jesus. Come, see the love of God displayed in its most surprising and powerful colors; come, learn to love your Maker, dressed in the riches of His grace. And may your souls be fired with divine love till all your carnal fetters are melted off, till you exult in a divine liberty, till you lead captivity captive and reign and triumph over all your vicious affections that had so often before disquieted and enslaved you.

And here again we may take up a melancholy complaint, how few are there who are taught to regulate their passions by divine love! What wild work do these unruly powers make among mankind! How dreadfully do they carry away multitudes into mischief and ruin for want of this holy government! How very few have attained this heavenly gift, this sacred principle, this golden rein of universal influence that would hold in and guide and manage all the passions to glorious advantage!

Meditation: "But it is time now, O my soul, to call your thoughts away from the multitudes of mankind and to look carefully into yourself. There is reason enough for grief and lamentation indeed if we survey the thousands round about us who are mere slaves to their earthly passions, who let them loose among creatures, and show very few tokens and evidences of a supreme love to their Creator. But would it not be matter of far more painful, more penetrating, and inward sorrow if you should carry this evidence, this test of divine love, into your own retirements and should hardly be able to prove yourself a lover of God? Awake, awake to the work, O my heart! Inquire, examine, and take a strict account how your passionate powers are employed. Go over your various affections and inquire of all of them, How stands your love to God?*

---

* Watts, *Works*, 2:652–53.

LOGICK:

OR,

THE RIGHT USE OF REASON

IN THE

ENQUIRY AFTER TRUTH.

WITH

A VARIETY OF RULES TO GUARD AGAINST ERROR IN THE AFFAIRS OF RELIGION
AND HUMAN LIFE, AS WELL AS IN THE SCIENCES.

Watts's publication on logic was widely used in academics across England and America. Yale College used it as the standard textbook on logic until at least the early nineteenth century.

29

Meditation

How necessary and useful a practice it is for a Christian to meditate often on the transcendent perfection and worth of the blessed God, to survey His attributes and His grace in Christ Jesus, to keep up in the mind a constant idea of His supreme excellence and frequently to repeat and confirm the choice of Him as our highest hope, our portion, and our everlasting good! This will keep the love of God warm at the heart and maintain the divine affection in its primitive life and vigor. But if our idea of the adorable and supreme excellence of God grow faint and feeble and sink lower in the mind; if we lose the sight of His amiable glories, the sense of His amazing love in the gospel, His rich promises and His alluring grace; if our will does not cleave to Him as our chief good and does not live on Him daily as our spring of happiness, we will abate the fervency of this sacred passion and our love to God will grow cold by degrees and suffer great and guilty decays.

How greatly and eternally are we indebted to Jesus, the Son of God, who has revealed the Father to us in all His most amiable characters and glories and brought Him, as it were, within the reach of our love! The three great springs of love to God are e: a clear discovery of what God is in Himself; a lively sense of what He has done for us; and a well-grounded hope of what He will bestow on us. All these are owed chiefly to our blessed Jesus. Let us consider them distinctly.

First, it is He, even the beloved Son of God, who lay in the bosom of the Father, who has made a fuller and brighter discovery to us what God is, what an admirable and transcendent being, a spirit glorious in all perfections. It is true, the light of nature dictates some of these things to us, and the ancient prophets have given further manifestations. But none knows the Father so as the Son does and those to whom the Son will reveal Him (Matt. 11:27). That blessed person, who is one with the Father, must know Him best, that illustrious man who is so intimately united to God and in whom "dwelleth all the fulness of the Godhead bodily" (Col. 2:9). He whose name is "Emmanuel...God with us" (Matt. 1:23), or God "manifest in the flesh" (1 Tim. 3:16)—He must know the Father with such an exquisite knowledge as far transcends the reach of all our ideas.

Let it be noted also that the blessed Jesus came down from heaven not only to show God all glorious to men but to make Him appear all lovely and desirable in the eyes of sinners by representing Him in all the wonders of His compassion and forgiving mercy. Even a great, a just, and a holy God is lovely and amiable in the sight of guilty creatures when He is willing to reconcile the world to Himself in and by His Son, Jesus Christ, not imputing to them their iniquities (2 Cor. 5:19). Such a sight of God is the first attraction of our love.

Second, it is the Son of God who came to inform us what God has done for us and thereby to engage our love. The reason of man and our daily experience teach us that He is the author of our being and our blessings. He causes the sun to shine and His rain to descend on the earth (Matt. 5:45); He gives us fruitful seasons and fills our hearts with food and gladness (Acts 14:17). But it is Jesus who has told us the eternal counsels of His Father's love and what kind designs He formed for our recovery from sin and hell.*

---

* Watts, *Works*, 2:639.

30

Prayer

First, how may we know when a soul gets near the seat of God in prayer? I answer, there will be some or all these attendants of nearness to God.

There will be an inward sense of the several glories of God and suitable exercises of grace in the soul. For when we are quite near to God, we see Him; we are in His presence. He is then, as it were, before the eyes of the soul, even as the soul is at all times before the eyes of God. There will be something of such a spiritual sense of the presence of God as we will have when our souls are dismissed from the prison of this flesh and we see Him face-to-face, though in a far less degree. It is something that resembles the future vision of God in the blessed world of spirits, and those souls who have had much intimacy with God in prayer will tell you that they know, in some measure, what heaven is.

The soul, when it gets near to God—even to His seat—beholds several of His glories displayed there, for it is a seat of majesty, a seat of judgment, and a seat of mercy. Under these three characters is the seat of God distinguished in Scripture. When the soul gets near to God, it sees Him as on a seat of majesty. There He appears to the soul in the first notion of His divinity or Godhead, as self-sufficient and the first of beings. He appears there as the infinite ocean, the immeasurable fountain of being and perfection and blessedness; and the soul, in a due exercise of grace, shrinks, as it were, into nothing before Him as a drop or a dust, a mere atom of being. The soul is in its own eyes at that time what it is always in the eyes of God—as nothing and less than nothing and vanity. He appears then in the glory of His all-sufficiency as an almighty Creator, giving birth and life and being to all things; and the soul, in a due exercise of grace, stands before Him as a dependent creature, receiving all its powers and being from Him, supported every moment by Him, and ready to sink into utter nothing if God withdraw that support. Such is God, and such is the soul when the soul draws near to God in worship.

He appears again on His seat of majesty as a sovereign, in the glory of His infinite supremacy, and the soul sees Him as the supreme of beings, owns His just sovereignty, and subjects itself afresh and forever to His high dominion. O with what deep humility and self-abasement does the saint, considered merely as a creature, cast himself down at the foot of God when he comes near to the seat of His majesty! "Behold," says Abraham, "I now have taken upon me to speak unto Thee, I who am but dust and ashes" (see Gen. 18:27). This is the language of a saint when got near to the seat of the majesty of God: "Before I had seen You as such a sovereign, I was restive and stubborn: in times past I quarreled with God because of difficult duties imposed on me and because of the difficult dispensations I was made to pass through, but now I behold God so infinitely my superior that I can quarrel no more with any duty or any difficulty; I submit to all His will. Whatsoever He will have me be, that I am; whatsoever He bids me do, that I do, for it is fit He should be a sovereign and I should be a subject. I give myself to Him afresh and forever, that He may dispose of me according to His own will and for His own glory. I would be more regardless of myself and more regardful of my God. It is fit He should be the ultimate end of all that I can be and all that I can do, for He is my sovereign."*

* Watts, *Works*, 1:52–53.

31

Worship

This part of my discourse leads me to consider the blessed difference that there will be between a Christian's appearing before God in heaven, and his appearance here in divine ordinances before God on earth. And by a comparison of these two, may the Spirit of God awaken our faith, our hope, our love, and our joy, and all join to promote our sanctification! The differences then between our standing before God in worship now and our worshiping before God in heaven are such as these.

First, now the true Christian appears in a mixed assembly of saints and sinners. There the assembly is all holy, and not one sinner among them. Here sincere souls and hypocrites meet together in worship; there the hypocrite is forever banished. In the houses of God on earth, the wicked Canaanites will mingle with the children of Israel, but in His temple in heaven, everyone is an Israelite indeed. There will no more be found a "Canaanite in the house of the LORD of hosts" (Zech. 14:21).

Second, in this world the saint appears among a few to worship his God, but then among millions. Now many times we have worshiped in a secret corner for fear of men, but then it is all in public glory. For there all the worship that is paid is the established worship of the whole country, and honors and kingdoms and wealth are all on that side. All the inhabitants are made rich forever with the riches of heaven. And all the children of God are the sons and daughters of a king, and all heirs and possessors of glory, and reign together with the Lord Jesus (Rom. 8:17; 2 Tim. 2:12).

Third, now we worship in a way of preparation; there for enjoyment and full delight. Ordinances here are but slight shadows and very faint and imperfect resemblances of what the worship in heaven will be. Now the word of God is spoken by a man, and it loses much of the divinity and power by the means of conveyance; there it will be spoken by God Himself to our spirits or by our Lord Jesus Christ to the ears of our bodies, raised, sanctified, and immortal. And our souls will receive as much of the express ideas as God designs to convey by all His conversation with that sanctified number. Nor will they miss any of the beauty or spirit or perfection of those thoughts that God Himself would impress on us.

Fourth, now we appear with imperfect services and poor improvements; there with glorious and complete worship. For here we see God but as in "a glass, darkly; but then face to face" (1 Cor. 13:12). Now we can have His glory or His grace represented to us but in part, in a small measure, and according to our poor capacities of receiving; there we will see Him as He is and know as we are known.

Fifth, I might say that we come with very little comfort and many discouragements to appear before God on earth, but there with everlasting consolation. We come now to the Word and we go away again, hardly hearing the voice of God in His Word or seeing His countenance, but there we will be forever near Him, with no wall of flesh or of sin to divide us.

Last, now we appear and depart again, but then we will abide with God forever. Now we go down from the mount of converse with God into the world of temptation and sin and business and care. We appear on Mount Horeb or Pisgah, and we take a little view of the promised land; but we go down again, as the children of Israel did, to fight with the Canaanites, the giants that are in the valley, our mighty sins, our strong corruptions. In this valley of tears we must have a conflict before we get to the promised land; there, every worshiper has in his hand a palm of complete victory (Rev. 7:9), and he is forever discharged from fighting. "Him that overcometh will I make a pillar in the temple of my God, and he shall go no more out" (Rev. 3:12).*

---

* Watts, *Works*, 1:157–60.

Cotton Mather (1663–1728)
The New England Puritan was responsible for
helping introduce Watts's hymns and poems to
America by appending them to printed sermons
and prayers.

32

The Lord's Supper

The Lord's Supper Instituted

'Twas on that dark, that doleful night
When powers of earth and hell arose
Against the Son of God's delight,
And friends betray'd Him to His foes.

Before the mournful scene began
He took the bread and blest and brake.
What love thro' all His actions ran!
What wondrous words of grace He spake!

"This is My body broke for sin,
Receive and eat the living food."
Then took the cup and blest the wine;
"'Tis the new cov'nant in My blood."

For us His flesh with nails was torn,
He bore the scourge, He felt the thorn;
And justice pour'd upon His head
Its heavy vengeance in our stead.

For us His vital blood was spilt,
To buy the pardon of our guilt,
When for black crimes of biggest size
He gave His soul a sacrifice.

"Do this" (He cried) "'till time shall end,
In memory of your dying Friend;
Meet at My table, and record
The love of your departed Lord."

Jesus, Thy feast we celebrate,
We show Thy death, we sing Thy name,
Till Thou return, and we shall eat
The marriage supper of the Lamb.

Our Lord Jesus at His Own Table
The memory of our dying Lord
Awakes a thankful tongue.
How rich He spread His royal board,
And blest the food, and sung.

Happy the men that eat this bread,
But double blest was he
That gently bow'd his loving head,
And lean'd it, Lord, on thee.

By faith the same delights we taste
As that great favorite did,
And sit and lean on Jesus's breast,
And take the heavenly bread.

Down from the palace of the skies
Hither the King descends,
"Come, my beloved, eat" (He cries),
"And drink salvation, friends.

"My flesh is food and physic too,
A balm for all your pains.
And the red streams of pardon flow
From these My pierced veins."

Hosanna to His bounteous love
For such a taste below!
And yet He feeds His saints above
With nobler blessings too.

Come the dear day, the glorious hour
That brings our souls to rest!
Then we shall need these types no more,
But dwell at th' heavenly feast.*

---

* Watts, *Works*, 4:347, 351–52.

33

Virtue

Virtue is an honorable and extensive name. It is used by moral writers to include all the duties we owe to ourselves or to our fellow creatures, such as sobriety, temperance, faithfulness, justice, prudence, goodness, and mercy. And the sense of it is sometimes stretched so far as to comprehend also the duties of religion that we owe to God. But let us take notice that the first and original signification of the word both in the Greek and Latin tongues is much more limited, and it means only "power" or "courage." The Greek word used here [i.e., "virtue" in Phil. 4:8] by the apostle is derived from the name of Mars, or the heathen god of war. And doubtless the most ancient meaning of it among the Greek writers was "warlike valor," though in time the philosophers enlarged the sense of it to include every moral excellence.

The several places in the New Testament where the word is used have chief reference to some work of glorious power when it is applied to God, or courage when it refers to men. I wish I could stay here to explain them all, but I must mention one of them, 2 Peter 1:5–6: "Add to your faith virtue; and to virtue knowledge, and to knowledge temperance." Virtue is to be added to faith—that is, next to your belief of the gospel, get courage to profess what you believe.

It is not to be supposed that in this place *virtue* can signify the whole of morality because the particular virtues of temperance, patience, and charity are named also. And therefore this must signify some part of morality distinct from the rest—namely, a strength or fortitude of soul.

And for the same reason, the word *virtue* in Philippians 4:8 cannot signify the whole system of moral duties because St. Paul in the same verse had been recommending truth, justice, and purity or temperance, which are so many pieces of morality; and it is not reasonable to imagine that he brings in a general name that comprehends them all in the midst of so many particulars, which is contrary to the use of all writers and to his own custom too. I confess that if he had said, "if there be any other virtue," we might then have understood *virtue* in the general sense. But now it is evident that he means a particular excellence, distinct from those mentioned, and the word itself requires us to understand a brave, bold, and generous spirit and practice. He recommends to them a great and excellent behavior wherein their holy courage may appear when the call of providence gives a just occasion.

Courage is a virtue that stands in opposition to both fear and shame, and it guards the mind of man from the evil influence of both those passions. The man of courage has not such a feeling of fondness for his flesh or his estate as to be afraid to profess his sentiments or to fulfill his duty at every call of providence, though his estate may suffer damage by it or his flesh be exposed to pain. Nor has he such tenderness for his honor as to secure it with the loss of his innocence. He is not ashamed to appear for virtue in an age of vice and scandal. He stands up boldly for the honor of his God and ventures a thousand perils rather than wound his conscience or betray his trust. He dares profess and practice temperance among a herd of drunkards, and purity in the midst of the lewd and unclean. The man of courage can despise the threatenings of the great and the scoffs of the witty, conscious of his own integrity and truth. He can face and oppose the world with all its terrors and travel onward in the paths of piety without fear. The righteous man is bold as a lion (Prov. 28:1).*

---

* Watts, *Works*, 1:316–17.

Philip Doddridge (1702–1751)
The nonconformist minister, educator, and hymn writer was one of Watts's closest friends and compiled Watts's complete works for publication after his death.

34

Friendship

How well has the blessed God provided for love and union among all His true worshipers! He has left them no just ground to contend and quarrel or break themselves into little angry parties, for He has now appointed but one religion for them all, one general method of access to Him. He has ordained but one Mediator, Jesus Christ, and has appointed one Spirit to draw their hearts near to Himself. A glorious religion indeed that unites Jews and Gentiles and mankind of all nations to the great and blessed God! And what a disgrace is it to this religion that we should not be more united to one another! We "are no more strangers and foreigners, but fellowcitizens with the saints, and of the household of God" (Eph. 2:19).

What a most absurd and grievous thing it is that we who are brought into such a state of friendship by divine grace should obey the corrupt dictates of nature and the lusts of the flesh! That we should quarrel and fight, even in the presence of that God to whom we have access by the blood of one Mediator and by the influence of one Spirit! Surely this must be a Spirit of union and peace and love, this one Spirit who reconciles God and man, who were at a dreadful distance; this Spirit who reconciles Jew and Gentile, who were mutual strangers and enemies.

And how can we suppose we are governed by this uniting Spirit—this Spirit of gentleness, meekness, and friendship—if we indulge the ferments of wrath and revenge in our bosom, if we resolve to carry on strife and contention with the language of railing and reviling against those who worship the same God by the same Mediator? How can we hope that this Spirit has ever reconciled us to God if we persist in enmity against our brethren? Should we have all faith and remove mountains, if we have not love, we are not Christians (1 Cor. 13:2). The very nature and life of Christianity is faith working by love, faith leading the soul to God the Father through the mediation of Jesus Christ His Son by the aid of the Holy Spirit and producing all works of holiness by the influence of love to God and man. May this be wrought in our hearts and practiced in our whole course of life.*

---

* Watts, *Works*, 1:496.

Jonathan Edwards (1703–1758)

The New England pastor-theologian was a contemporary of Watts and interacted with him through writing. Watts was instrumental in publishing and writing the preface for Edwards's *A Faithful Narrative*.

Reading Watts

Even though Watts's sermons, essays, and other miscellaneous writings are a substantial portion of his
contribution to applied Christianity and the spiritual
life, there has been little modern publication of these
materials. It was in 1753 that the first complete works
of Watts (sermons, dissertation, letters, and poetry)
were collected and published in six volumes by his
friends David Jennings and Philip Doddridge. This
first edition of Watts's works is no longer in print and
remains difficult to access. In 1810 these six volumes
were republished with memoirs added by George
Burder.[1] The 1810 publication, which is the source
for the excerpts in this book, is accessible digitally
on the internet and through various public domain
or internet archive sites. The Banner of Truth Trust
published one of Watts's writings related to the practice of prayer, *A Guide to Prayer*.[2] This work is Watts's

---

1. Isaac Watts, *The Works of the Late Reverend and Learned Isaac
Watts, D.D. Containing, Besides His Sermons and Essays on Miscellaneous
Subjects Several Additional Pieces, Selected from His Manuscripts by the Rev.
Dr. Jennings, and the Rev. Dr. Doddridge, in 1753 to Which are Prefixed,
Memoirs of the Life of the Author Compiled by the Rev. George Burder*
(London: J. Barfield, 1810).

2. Isaac Watts, *A Guide to Prayer* (Edinburgh: Banner of Truth,
2001).

most comprehensive and systematic approach to the prayer life of the Christian.

There are a number of biographies of Watts that are helpful examinations of his life, thought, and writings. Three are especially noteworthy. First, Arthur Paul Davis's *Isaac Watts: His Life and Works* is one of the better full-length biographies that is beneficial for understanding the controversies occurring in Watts's day and how Watts deals with them in his various works.[3] Second, Graham Beynon's *Isaac Watts: His Life and Thought* is the most recent biographical work on Watts.[4] Beynon interacts well with Watts's writings and aids the interested reader in better understanding his life and theology. Finally, Douglas Bond's *The Poetic Wonder of Isaac Watts* gives brief insight into Watts's life, with specific attention paid to his hymns and poetry.[5]

For those interested in a more scholarly engagement of Watts's theology, two more recent monographs on Watts have been published. First, Graham Beynon's work *Isaac Watts: Reason, Passion and the Revival of Religion* is a rigorous and beneficial study.[6] Beynon examines how Watts builds on an English Puritan heritage to navigate and engage the contours of his Enlightenment context. Beynon

---

3. Arthur Paul Davis, *Isaac Watts: His Life and Works* (London: Independent Press, 1943).

4. Graham Beynon, *Isaac Watts: His Life and Thought* (Fern, Rothshire, Scotland: Christian Focus, 2013).

5. Douglas Bond, *The Poetic Wonder of Isaac Watts* (Sanford, Fla.: Reformation Trust, 2013).

6. Graham Beynon, *Isaac Watts: Reason, Passion and the Revival of Religion* (London: Bloomsbury T&T Clark, 2016).

effectively clarifies how Watts aimed to revive religion in his day through the practical aspects of Christianity such as preaching, praise, and prayer. Second, *A Soul Prepared for Heaven: The Theological Foundation of Isaac Watts' Spirituality* is a deeper dive into the general outline of this edited volume.[7] The work takes a judicious approach to examining Watts's theological vision for the Christian spiritual life.

---

7. W. Britt Stokes, *A Soul Prepared for Heaven: The Theological Foundation of Isaac Watts' Spirituality*, Reformed Historical Theology, vol. 72 (Göttingen, Germany: Vandenhoeck & Ruprecht, 2022).